Addiction

Questions and Answers for Counsellors and Therapists

Addiction

Questions and Answers for Counsellors and Therapists

Edited by

BILL READING RMN, MA, Dip SocSci, Dip Dyn Psych
East Kent Community Alcohol Service

and

MICHAEL JACOBS MA(Oxon), FBAC
Psychotherapy and Counselling Consultant

W
WHURR PUBLISHERS
LONDON AND PHILADELPHIA

© 2003 Whurr Publishers

First published 2003 by
Whurr Publishers Ltd
19b Compton Terrace, London N1 2UN, England
325 Chestnut Street, Philadelphia PA19106, USA

British Library Cataloguing in Publication Data

A catalogue record for this book is available from the British
Library.

ISBN 1 86156 333 7

Printed and bound in the UK by Athenaeum Press Limited,
Gateshead, Tyne & Wear.

Contents

Chapter 6   124

Controlling drug and alcohol use

Contributors

Chris Cook is Professor of the Psychiatry of Alcohol Misuse at the University of Kent at Canterbury. His research interests include the genetics of alcohol misuse and spirituality and addiction. He is a consultant psychiatrist in East Kent and for the UK Civil Aviation Authority. He is an ordained priest in the Church of England. Professor Cook has published a variety of articles on addictions and related topics. With Professor Griffith Edwards and Dr Jane Marshall, he is co-author of *The Treatment of Drinking Problems*, Cambridge University Press, 1997.

Neil Hunt has been conducting research concerning drug use and health for more than ten years. He is a Lecturer in Addictive Behaviour at the University of Kent, Director of Research for KCA (UK) and a founder member of the UK Harm Reduction Alliance, which campaigns for healthy drug policy.

Paul Jackson is a BACP registered counsellor and works as a nurse-therapist at Mount Zeehan Alcohol Unit in Canterbury. He has published previous articles and chapters relating to motivational enhancement therapy and the counselling process within the addictions.

Rose Kent has a Masters degree in Social Work and is a chartered counselling psychologist. She has worked in a variety of non-statutory organizations for alcohol and drug users, as lecturer in Addictions Counselling at the University of Kent, and independently as a trainer, counsellor, supervisor and consultant. She is currently Training Co-ordinator for the Prevention of Professional Abuse Network (POPAN).

Bill Plummer is the consultant psychiatrist for the East Kent Community Alcohol Service. He has previously worked as a general practitioner and as a general psychiatrist, and has experience with counselling and psychotherapy in a wide variety of medical settings.

Bill Reading is manager of the East Kent Community Alcohol Service. He has trained counsellors and therapists for many years, including students at the University of Kent at Canterbury, where he is an honorary lecturer. He is a UKCP registered psychoanalytic psychotherapist.

Martin Weegmann is consultant clinical psychologist and group analyst for the Substance Misuse Service and Psychotherapy Department, Central and North West Thames Mental Health Trust.

Acknowledgements

Bill Reading would like to thank those students, clients and colleagues whose input has been both inspirational and challenging over the years – especially those associated with Mount Zeehan and the University of Kent. Much gratitude too to Pam Forrest for her administrative support and patience. Finally, thanks to three wise men, all currently in various modes of retirement, yet whose ideas have found their way into these pages – Alan Cartwright, Ron McKechnie and Terry Spratley.

CHAPTER 1
Introduction

Counsellors and therapists working in generic settings inevitably find themselves with clients or patients who present particular issues in which the therapist may have no particular or specialist training. Such occasions can be at the start of counselling, where a referral to a specialized agency is a possibility. They may also be some sessions into therapy, when issues are discussed or are recognized by the counsellor that may highlight the need for specialist advice but may not necessarily entail passing the client on. At these times it is valuable for counsellors, therapists and their supervisors to have access to those with particular expertise, so that they can continue to work with the client or can decide if specialist help is required.

This book is written with several types of reader in mind. It is intended primarily as a source of help for established counsellors and therapists who wish to enhance their capacity to offer help to those affected by problematic drug use. It will be of help also to those studying to become counsellors and therapists. We hope that it will also appeal to those who may wish to enquire further into the process of counselling those who use drugs, whatever the reasons for their curiosity.

Although this book addresses the general question of counselling those with 'addiction', the contributors have taken the use of mind-altering substances as being their central focus; nonetheless, much of what is written here will be of relevance to those behaviours that do not involve the use of drugs yet which may qualify for the label of 'addiction', such as gambling. Much of the content of the answers to the questions contained in this book offers practical advice on how to be more helpful to those of our clients who use drugs. However, it is also our intention to raise questions about the very use of the term 'addiction'. We wish also to encourage readers to give priority to the experiences and concerns of clients

1

with whom they may come into contact, rather than engaging in ideology, since this may cloud our ability to see clearly the client before us and his or her presenting problems.

There are few examples in history in which cultures have not used intoxicants, and there is nothing to suggest that this trend is likely to diminish in the future. This book collects together the thinking of writers whose major experience of the addictions has taken place within the United Kingdom, although much of what is contained here has international validity. We exist in a context in which drug use is routine, and where problems arising from and linked to drug use are to be expected. The authors whose work comprises this book are united in the view that people who experience problems related to drug use are precisely that – people who experience problems related to drug use. Furthermore, it is our contention that we know what comprises good counselling and therapeutic intervention, both in terms of that which is likely to succeed and that which is ethically sound. It is our suggestion that effective and ethical practice with drug-using clients is subject to the same principles that underpin good counselling and therapeutic engagement with all clients, namely a good context in which to work, a competent and committed counsellor or therapist, and a client who is free to decide whether or not to engage in the relationship and enjoy its potential rewards.

The apparently harmful use of drugs and/or alcohol often seems contradictory and counter-intuitive. Perhaps for these reasons, the processes that we may term 'addictions' invite a huge number of potential explanatory models and proffered solutions, with some of these featuring in the pages to follow. Indeed, some models of understanding seem to advocate views of drug-users that render them no longer subject to the usual rules of human experience, or which deny them the ability to engage in high quality counselling and therapy. The authors of this volume cannot claim to be free of ideologies or even prejudice, although we would argue (of course!) that our own prejudices are preferable to those of some others who offer their views on addiction!

There is a contemporary pressure on counsellors and therapists to demonstrate the 'evidence-base' for what they do with clients, with or without the assistance of formal research, as a means of attempting to prove their effectiveness. Study and research into the content of various treatment approaches has thus far failed to reveal any significant and reliable difference between those approaches that seem to work at all. However, we now have several decades of research that is robust in demonstrating that the process of counselling and therapy is highly significant in shaping its eventual effectiveness. More specifically, we are able to see that in both generic and substance-misuse-specific counselling and therapy, it is the therapist variables that have a consistent bearing on engagement, retention and eventual outcome in counselling. Much of what is written within this book pays homage to the repeated finding that those therapists who are able to express a genuine sense of therapeutic commitment tend to have more productive relationships with their clients. Indeed, it can be argued that therapists and counsellors who offer themselves as warm, caring and genuine individuals to their clients offer a better quality of experience, one which deserves acknowledgement independently of its potential correlation with 'measurable' outcomes, such as reductions in drug use, improved social functioning or better physical health.

In selecting the questions that we have attempted to answer in the book, we have been able to draw on many years of experience in both clinical and academic environments, and to select those questions that we have most often been asked by non-specialist colleagues, particularly those already established in providing counselling and psychotherapy. There is little doubt that some clients will continue to need the services of specialist drug and alcohol services, although this may often be provided in tandem with ongoing therapy elsewhere. It is our hope that this volume will provide generic practitioners with an enhanced ability to be able to work with clients who use drugs, regardless of whether or not such drug use is identified as being problematic. Those who offer counselling and therapy in non-specialist settings are likely to see clients whose drug use ranges from being minimal to being a major factor in their lives. It is our view that drug use is best regarded as functional and as having meaning within the life of the client. Most counsellors are good listeners, and it is our hope that our answers will extend the ability of counsellors to listen to the drug-related experiences of their clients. We are perhaps suggesting that whatever differences might exist between drug-using clients and those who do not use drugs are primarily quantitative rather than qualitative in nature. Attempts to demonstrate the effectiveness of generalized approaches to counselling stand in clear danger of hindering the very processes that lie at the heart of good counselling and psychotherapy, most specifically the uniquely personal experience that takes place between counsellor and client, which should be meaningful and rewarding to both parties.

Although drug use may sometimes seem to be perplexing, and a potential source of insecurity for counsellors, we hope that we will succeed in helping our readers enjoy the tremendous personal reward and satisfaction that we know to be possible in our work with so-called 'addicted' clients. Such satisfaction lies at the heart of the counsellor's capacity for true therapeutic commitment. Those who use drugs may be able to be quite specific in terms of the changes they would like to make in their lives. It is the crucial skill of the counsellor and therapist to be able to facilitate the achievement of such goals while respecting at all times the autonomy of the client.

> I think that therapy is most effective when the therapist's goals are limited to the process of therapy and not to the outcome. I think that if the therapist feels 'I want to be present to this person as much as possible. I want to listen to what is going on. I want to be real in this relationship' then these are suitable goals for the therapist. If the therapist is feeling 'I want this person to get over his neurotic behaviour. I want this person to change in such-and-such a way' I think this stands in the way of good therapy.

> (Carl Rogers, *The Use of the Self in Therapy*, cited in Bragan 1996: 108)

CHAPTER 2

Understanding and assessing drinking and drug use

2.1 Why do people take drugs?

Trying to understand human behaviour is a complex and confusing task. The difficulties are even more marked when we question drug use, since such behaviour defies easy explanation. For example, an individual using drugs is often able to recognize harmful consequences yet continues to use them despite this awareness. A further difficulty arises because this question 'Why?' invites a series of supplementary questions, for example:

'Why does this woman use drugs?'   'Because she likes the effect of drugs.'
'Why does she like the effect of drugs?'   'Because it feels nice.'
'Why does it feel nice?'   'Because . . . , etc.'

Nevertheless, the attempt to understand why one person uses drugs in a particular way is of tremendous importance, both in terms of assessing what help may be necessary in order to promote change and, perhaps more fundamentally, enabling the counsellor to engage empathically in relating to an aspect of the client's experience which may continue to hold powerful significance even in the face of repeated adverse consequences of drug use.

A more practical and helpful means of addressing this question is to consider what factors are likely to influence whether or not an individual takes drugs, and the way in which drugs are likely to be taken. The following categorization applies to those using drugs both problematically and non-problematically. It provides a means through which the counsellor is able to construct an understanding of the factors that determine the way in which a client uses drugs. It is a model which can be shared explicitly with clients, and that may help to form a mutual basis for understanding within the therapeutic alliance.

5

This model comprises three categories of factors which are invariably and crucially interlinked but which can be separated for the purpose of enabling an enhanced understanding of the processes involved. The categories affecting drug use are:

(a) situational factors
(b) personal factors
(c) adaptational factors.

Situational factors

This category refers to those generalized contexts in which drug use is likely to take place. Essentially, these factors refer to the external environment, and tend to exert a similar influence on all those exposed to such environments. Situational factors can be broken down into five principal sub-categories.

The availability of drugs

This is clearly the most important situational factor, in that no drug use can occur if drugs are not available. Conversely, drug use is shown to increase in situations where a particular drug is readily available. Most generally, it is not only consumption that increases when drugs are available but also the incidence of harm associated with the use of a particular drug. As with all other situational factors, individuals may modify their situations in ways that either increase or decrease the availability of drugs, with consequent effects upon their consumption of drugs and the tendency to experience harm.

For the client who wishes to reduce drug use, minimizing exposure to situations in which drugs are available may have an important part to play in the overall strategy. Conversely, clients may find themselves gravitating towards situations in which drugs are more readily available with quite different consequences. It is often the case that increasing exposure to situations of high availability occurs without the client being fully aware of what is happening.

The price of drugs

Although it is not possible to draw a strict linear relation between price and consumption of drugs, the relative price of drugs tends to exert an influence on consumption. Cheaper drugs are likely to be associated with increased consumption. Consumption tends to reduce where the price of the drug becomes prohibitive. Once again, individuals are far from passive when it comes to the price of drugs; and those who wish to use drugs more heavily may engage in life-changes that essentially lead to getting more money in order to purchase drugs. Additionally, the individual may adopt drug-taking practices that maximize the cost-effectiveness of those drugs that are consumed, e.g. drinking cheaper forms of alcohol, or injecting rather than inhaling heroin.

The effects of control

Individuals tend to consume drugs less in situations where external control on consumption is in effect. Conversely, consumption of drugs is likely to increase where there is little or no external control upon the person's consumption. Although there are clearly situations in which prohibitive attitudes to drugs may be seen to increase their attractiveness, external control remains a very potent factor in limiting consumption. Once again, individual consumers of drugs may be quite active in either increasing or decreasing their susceptibility to external control. For example, drug-takers may develop lifestyles which remove them from the potential control of others; conversely, they may choose to enter into situations in which control is exercised 'on their behalf', as is the case in many residential drug-treatment facilities.

Encouragement to use drugs

Certain situations exert encouragement to use drugs or to use them more heavily. For example, membership of certain sub-groups may require drug use of those who wish to claim membership of such groups. Particular social gatherings may also encourage use of particular drugs, e.g. the use of ecstasy in the current 'dance culture', or the increased use of alcohol by those attending a wedding party.

Again, it is useful to consider the ways in which individuals may be active in exposing themselves to situations in which drug use is encouraged rather than discouraged. It is often the case that an individual drug-user has decreasing contact with those who do not use drugs in a similar fashion, with a corresponding tendency to increase contact with those who do.

Learning

Exposure to the ways in which other people use drugs provides an important source of learning for any given individual. This may occur in the early years of life where exposure to parental or familial use of drugs may provide a model for later personal drug use, or in contemporary situations within which 'social learning' takes place. We know that children who have been raised in drug-taking and drinking environments have an increased chance of using drugs and alcohol heavily in their own lives. Sadly this sometimes seems to occur even when such early exposures have been quite negative in character. This is not to suggest that those who have observed more drug use by others will inevitably increase their own consumption of drugs. There are many situations in which the impact of such learning is to produce aversive and avoidant attitudes to drug use by a particular individual. As counsellors and therapists, we have a special interest in understanding the ways in which past and current experiences with others shape the individual's perceptions and behaviours. Helping the client to understand the ways in which behaviours may have a 'learned component' may have an important part to play in assisting the client in the process of 'unlearning', and in the adoption of other ways in which these experiences can be managed.

In counselling, a good deal of emphasis is rightly placed upon the client's inner mental life, and ultimately on the unique way in which individuals manage their lives, including their use of drugs. However, an appreciation of the external factors that tend to influence drug use provides an invaluable context, in which the unique interplay between the client and his/her environment may be usefully explored. Such an understanding also offers a means of thinking about some of the factors that may need attention should the client be considering a change in drug use.

Personal factors

The personal factors affecting drug use obviously relate to the circumstances of particular individuals, in contrast to the more generalized situational factors that are described above. Personal factors may be considered under two headings: intrinsic factors and symbolic factors.

Intrinsic factors

These refer specifically to the effects of particular drugs for given individuals. To some degree, it is possible to think of the ways in which people use drugs in order to meet personal needs and dispositions, i.e. people tend to use specific drugs in order to obtain specific effects from them. Those who experience problematic anxiety may be inclined to use drugs which reduce anxiety, those with low esteem may use drugs which elevate self-esteem and those who experience feelings of deadness may use stimulant drugs which produce increased feelings of excitation and aliveness. Although specific groups of drugs have quite particular effects, it is important to note that different individuals may have quite different experiences from the same drug and that it is the understanding of the specific effects of the drug for an individual that is likely to be most helpful in working with that particular person.

The counsellor or therapist may discover that detailed, empathic exploration of the effects enjoyed as a result of drug use provides a valuable insight into, and a point of contact with, very important areas of the client's intimate experience. For example, we may come to understand that drugs have hitherto provided a much more reliable source of emotional supply than anything experienced in relation to other people. In turn, we may be able to help the client to understand the ways in which past relationships have been problematic and aim at improving the prospect for more successful relationships in the future.

Symbolic factors

Although intimately connected, symbolic factors differ from intrinsic factors in that they are concerned with the meaning of drug use for a particular individual. This meaning tends to be linked, first, to the individual's sense of identity and, second, to the meaning of drug use in the person's interpersonal relationships.

The ways in which drugs are taken inevitably have consequences for an individual's sense of personal identity. Some may rely on the use of a particular drug in order to maintain a sense of identity, particularly perhaps where other means of so doing are fragile. For some people, drug use may feature very high in the hierarchy of descriptors that create a personal sense of meaning and identity. It has been observed that even the fact that someone has a problem with a drug (including attempts to resolve the problem) may provide an important source of identity for some individuals. For example, being 'a (heavy) drinker' can be a means by which some men bolster their sense of masculinity, whereas the use of illicit drugs may be attractive to some of those who wish to foster a more rebellious self-image.

Secondly, drug use conveys meaning about a person's relationships with others. Such interpersonal symbolism may include wishing to 'belong' by sharing in drug-taking activities; or it may represent a means of expressing feelings such as hostility and defiance to others who may disapprove of drug use. It is sometimes difficult to separate symbolic effects that are interpersonal from those that relate to personal identity. For example, a client who finds it difficult to express anger may use alcohol in order to disinhibit emotionally and become more able to express angry feelings. Indeed, the act of drinking itself may convey important personal messages to those with whom the client may be feeling angry.

It often seems the case that clients may initially have a very limited understanding of the way in which drug use plays a part both in identity-formation and in communication with others. Sensitive counselling can rapidly enhance the client's capacity to appreciate some of the subtleties involved. The counsellor may be able to explore counter-transference feelings as a means of understanding some of the 'meta-messages' associated with a client's drug use. For example, the counsellor may become aware of feelings of disapproval, where the client's drug use seems to oppose the capacity for working together within the therapeutic alliance.

Adaptational factors

In using the term 'adaptational factors' we refer to those changes which have occurred as a result of previous drug use, and which themselves become factors in sustaining and promoting further use of the drug (see Figure 2.1). Such factors often take the form of 'vicious cycles' and can occur in almost all conceivable aspects of the client's functioning and experience.

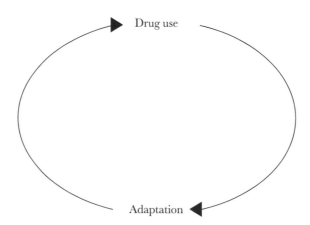

Figure 2.1. A simple model of the role of adaptational factors.

For the purposes of illustration, we outline adaptations in three areas: physical adaptation; adaptation of belief systems; and lifestyle adaptations.

Physical adaptations

Some drug users become increasingly tolerant to the drugs they are using (see also Question 2.7). Essentially, this means that increased quantities of the drug are required in order to achieve the desired effect (see Figure 2.2).

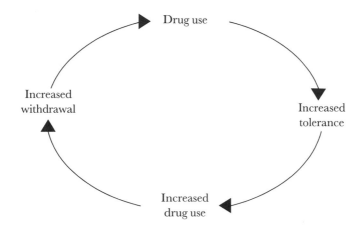

Figure 2.2. A cycle of physical adaptation.

Additionally, individuals may find that they experience withdrawal symptoms, and then discover that resumed use of the drug relieves such symptoms, at least temporarily.

Thus an individual may use drugs more heavily because the desired effects will otherwise not occur. Consequently, he or she may find that heavier use brings about increasingly severe withdrawal symptoms that require further consumption of the drug in order to achieve relief or avoidance of such symptoms.

Adaptation of belief systems

To some extent, we all see the world in ways that concur with our existing mind-set. If an individual uses drugs regularly and finds them helpful/functional in daily life, it is easy to see the way in which belief systems start to adapt in order to accommodate to this situation. For example, a regular drug user becomes increasingly likely to perceive the world in terms that suggest that continued drug use is routine, necessary or even essential (see Figure 2.3).

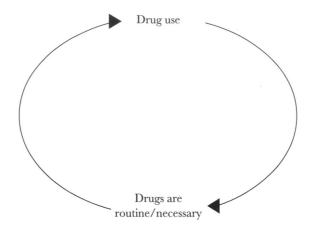

Figure 2.3. Adaptation of belief systems.

In counselling, a client may refer to the use of drugs in ways that suggest an unquestioning attitude: drugs are seen as 'something I needed', often requiring the client to ignore evidence that contradicts this view. A belief that drug use is 'necessary' is likely to incline the person towards continued drug use, particularly in situations where this belief is reinforced by the experience of repeated withdrawal symptoms.

Lifestyle adaptations

These factors cover a very broad range of possibilities. For example, a client who is using drugs may tend to associate more with others who use the same drugs and less with those who do not do so. This shift in social affiliation may itself become a factor in promoting continued drug use. Others may spend increasing proportions of disposable income to procure drugs, with consequent neglect of their other needs. A client may present with a lifestyle that no longer seems to have any source of comfort or satisfaction, other than that derived from drug use. Here again, such a position clearly disposes the individual to continued reliance upon drugs rather than upon other sources of satisfaction or comfort.

As indicated above, adaptational factors may occur in many areas. The examples cited above are inevitably interlinked, so that the experience of tolerance and withdrawal can affect beliefs about drug use, and such beliefs in turn can then lead to adaptations in lifestyle, etc.

Conclusion

Rather than asking 'Why does this person take drugs?', a more useful question is 'What are the factors that influence this person's use of drugs?' It is more helpful to think about personal drug use in terms of the model that is presented here. Experience suggests that this model lends itself readily to use with clients, both as a means for enhancing the counsellor's ability to understand better the client's drug use, and as a way of both client and counsellor working together towards those changes that become possible as a result of improved understanding.

Bill Reading

* * *

2.2 Why do some people develop problems whereas others seem not to?

In common with most things which people do, the use of drugs carries some degree of risk. Broadly speaking, the more an individual uses a particular drug, the more likely it is that he or she will experience certain forms of harm as a result. The same relation between the extent of drug use and the potential for harm may be observed across populations as well as in individuals. The prevalence of a particular drug-related problem within a society is likely to reflect the extent to which a particular drug is used within that society.

However, it is not sufficient to assert that all those using a particular drug in a particular way will experience the same harmful consequences. This question rightly asks why people with apparently similar patterns of drug use may have quite differing propensities to develop problems as a result of such use.

In addition to understanding the extent and manner of an individual's drug use, it is important to understand what makes one individual more vulnerable to problems than another using drugs in a similar fashion. The propensity to experience drug-related problems can be expressed in the following simple equation:

Pattern of drug use	+	Vulnerability to experience problems

=	Likelihood of experiencing drug-related problems

The interplay between the way in which drugs are used and the level of individual susceptibility to particular kinds of problems provides the basis for answering this question. Some patterns of drug use are universally harmful, e.g. extreme over-dosage and some problems of drug toxicity. The origins of some other drug-related harms may owe far more to the vulnerability factors affecting a given individual or group of individuals. One example is oriental flushing syndrome, a situation in which relatively small amounts of alcohol produce quite pronounced physiological effects in some vulnerable individuals (see Question 2.3). Another example occurs in those individuals with fragile personality organizations, who may be prone to experience harmful effects on behaviour and mood at relatively low levels of drug use. For these people, their psychological vulnerability places them at increased risk of experiencing harm, such as psychotic episodes or aggressive acting-out.

Some theoretical models place more reliance on 'vulnerability' factors than on actual consumption of drugs. For example, the Twelve Step model suggests that certain users of drugs are particularly prone to experience difficulty, rather than viewing drugs per se as responsible for the development of problems. Vulnerable individuals are seen as manifesting a pre-existing and enduring tendency to develop problems whenever drugs are used.

There are four principal ways in which the use of drugs is likely to cause problems: intoxication, withdrawal, toxicity and adaptation.

Intoxication

Problems may arise as the direct result of periods of intoxication, either in the short or long term. Increased risk of accidents or inappropriate social conduct are common examples of problems to which intoxication gives rise. Clearly the kinds of problems that may be encountered through intoxication tend to reflect the qualities of the particular drug that is being used (see Question 2.5).

The *context* in which intoxication occurs can also be a powerful determinant as to whether problems are likely to ensue. For example, intoxication is likely to have very different consequences depending upon whether the individual is in an appropriate social situation or behind the wheel of a car.

Toxicity

Some harm occurs as a result of the toxic or poisoning effects of drugs themselves and/or the means by which drugs are administered. 'Street heroin' often contains impurities that are quite dangerous whereas pure heroin seems to cause relatively little physical damage to those who take it. Alcohol is notorious in its ability to cause damage to almost all types of body tissue given sufficiently heavy consumption. Once again, the effects of toxicity may be acute or relatively long-term. Although rare, it is possible for a single dose of MDMA (ecstasy) to have fatal consequences, whereas some forms of alcoholic liver disease occur only after many years of heavy and frequent consumption.

Although not strictly a toxic effect, some drug use also carries the risk of infection, most obviously the introduction of blood-borne viruses such as hepatitis B/C or HIV as a result of unsatisfactory injecting practices. There is currently concern that the 'snorting' of drugs such as cocaine or amphetamine may also represent a means by which such infections may be transmitted and/or acquired.

Withdrawal

The effects of withdrawal from drugs may themselves be harmful. Some drugs such as alcohol and barbiturates can give rise to epileptic-type fits during the phase of withdrawal from them. It is not uncommon for people to become very depressed during the period of withdrawal from stimulants such as cocaine and amphetamines. Many people who smoke cigarettes probably do so primarily in order to stave off nicotine withdrawal, which otherwise gives rise to unpleasant feelings of discomfort and agitation (see Question 2.7).

Adaptation

The changes that individuals make in order to accommodate previous drug use can also give rise to different forms of harm. For some, engaging in illegal activities associated with drug use may result in a criminal record that can have very long-lasting consequences for the future. Those who become very highly tolerant to a particular drug may use increased quantities in order to achieve desired effects, thus risking the harmful consequences that are likely to accompany increases in consumption.

Conclusion

These different ways in which drugs may cause problems for some people and not others need to be seen as interlinked. When trying to understand why a particular person may have developed a problem, it can be extremely helpful to consider not only the pattern of drug use per se but also the factors which dispose that individual to develop a particular difficulty. Failure to acknowledge and respond to the vulnerabilities that may dispose a client to experience harm can give rise to a situation where further episodes of harm are more likely. The counselling relationship offers the potential to focus not only on potential changes to drug use, but also on those 'underlying' factors that may otherwise leave the client vulnerable to repeated problems in the future.

Bill Reading

* * *

2.3 I've been told that some people are genetically disposed to have 'addictive personalities'. Is there an accepted theory of addiction?

There have been many accepted theories of addiction, and some of these are more popular than others. However, it is difficult to justify any one of these as the accepted theory. This is partly because of the controversy that continues to rage in various areas, but it is also because there is a tendency towards reductionism, which focuses on narrow areas of scientific research in the hope of finding an underlying or foundational 'cause' for addiction. In fact, any serious attempt to understand the causes of addiction is a truly multi-dimensional quest, which of necessity must include biological, psychological, social and spiritual considerations.

People live in social and physical environments. Whatever degree of personal predisposition they may have towards addictive problems, they will clearly not express this predisposition if a focus for them does not exist in their surroundings. No one will become an alcoholic if they live in a totally alcohol-free environment and are never offered the opportunity to drink an alcoholic beverage. However, this immediately raises a question as to what a 'predisposition to addictive disorders' might be predisposing to. If the predisposition is specific to alcohol, for example, then clearly the presence of alcohol in the environment will be a key factor. On the other hand, if the predisposition is to a particular pattern of behaviour, perhaps independent of any particular substance or drug, then this can arise as an actual problem in virtually any environment.

In fact, we know that the availability and acceptability of alcohol is vitally important in determining the prevalence in any given community of alcohol-related problems of all kinds. Thus, the cheaper, more widely available and acceptable alcohol becomes, the more a community is likely to suffer from drink-driving offences, alcohol-related liver disease, alcohol-related accidents, alcohol-related marital disharmony and a whole range of other alcohol-related problems. At least to some extent, then, it would seem that there is a degree of environmental specificity in the development of disorders related to certain drugs within a community.

Similarly, there is good evidence for substance-specific predisposition to particular problems for particular individuals. For example, the so-called 'oriental flushing syndrome' is a genetically based disorder, which confers an impairment of alcohol metabolization on individuals who possess a particular mutation of the 'alcohol dehydrogenase gene'. When individuals who possess this mutation drink alcohol, they experience an aversive reaction that includes facial flushing as well as cardio-vascular disturbance. Such individuals are more likely to be abstainers or light social drinkers, and are thus at less risk of alcohol-related problems than others within the same community.

There are, therefore, apparently specific predispositions that occur by virtue of personal or environmental characteristics and that increase or reduce the likelihood of addiction to a specific substance. However, assuming a given environment, and allowing that the oriental flushing syndrome is rare in the Caucasian population, it would seem that many factors that confer an individual's predispositions have yet to be identified.

Amongst personal predisposing factors, a range of psychological traits has been considered important. Amongst these, a particularly popular hypothesis has been that of the 'addictive personality'. The notion inherent in this hypothesis appears to be that some people have personality traits that specifically predispose them to become addicted to any one of a range of substances or behaviours. According to the pure form of this hypothesis, the particular substance or behaviour that acts as the focus for addiction is relatively immaterial. Indeed, given appropriate circumstances, many addicts happily transfer their addictive behaviour from one substance or behaviour to another according to circumstances. This hypothesis is extremely persuasive for those who have worked in clinical services catering for addicts, as many clients in such services today are addicted to multiple substances, and often transfer their addictive behaviour from one substance to another. Similarly, a range of behavioural patterns that do not actually involve substance misuse have also been described as showing 'addictive' qualities. This appears to suggest that it is the behaviour of the individual that is the common underlying theme.

In fact, many of the traits of the supposedly 'addictive personality' are attributable to the consequences of addiction rather than its aetiology. Furthermore, although a range of personality traits have been shown to predispose to various addictive disorders, none of these traits appear to be specific to addictions. For example, antisocial personality traits or anxiety traits appear to place an individual at higher risk of alcohol misuse. However, many such individuals do not go on to experience problems with their drinking, and others develop different disorders, such as anxiety disorders or antisocial personality disorder.

There is increasing evidence, however, that there is a degree of individual predisposition to alcohol-related problems conferred on the basis of genetic factors. Exactly what these genetic factors might be is currently a subject of research and debate. Research from a wide range of different genetic methods (population studies, twin studies, adoption studies and genetic marker studies) has tended to support the hypothesis that there is a genetically transmitted predisposition towards both alcohol-related problems and other addictive disorders. This genetic predisposition may be specific to alcohol, as in the case of the oriental flushing syndrome; or it is possible that it confers a predisposition to a broader range of addictions.

In 1990, a group of American researchers found that a particular variant of a genetic marker at the 'D2 dopamine receptor gene locus' on chromosome 11 was present in 69 per cent of post-mortem samples from alcoholics, as compared with only 20 per cent of similar specimens from control subjects. Numerous subsequent publications concerning research in this field have produced varying results. Although some debate this view, there is overall good reason to believe that there is evidence of a genetic effect at this region of chromosome 11. Furthermore, other researchers have found that a similar association between this marker and polysubstance abuse, smoking, Gilles de la Tourette's syndrome, autism, attention-deficit hyperactivity disorder, and post-traumatic stress disorder. There is therefore some reason to believe that this genetic variation confers a predisposition to a range of disorders including not only addictions, but also a number of other fairly diverse diagnoses.

By far the largest genetic research study in this field is the American study known as the Collaboration on Genetics of Alcoholism (COGA). Preliminary results from this research suggest that regions of chromosomes 1 and 7 (and possibly chromosome 2) confer a genetic susceptibility to alcohol dependence. Conversely, on chromosome 4, a region has been identified that appears to confer a protective factor. It is likely that further results from this and other studies in the future will considerably enhance our understanding of those parts of the human genome that are specifically responsible for conferring a predisposition to alcohol misuse and alcohol dependence. Similarly, it is likely to become clear which inherited factors specifically affect alcohol problems, and which are relevant to a range of addictions or other disorders. It appears likely that a range of different genetic predispositions might eventually be identified. (See Cook and Gurling 2001: 257–79.)

Chris Cook

* * *

2.4 I have often heard reference to 'drug dependency'. What does this mean? Does it mean the same as 'being addicted' or 'having a problem'?

There are many ways in which we can try to understand the various phenomena that occur when people are using drugs regularly. More particularly, those who are using drugs often appear to behave in ways which seem contradictory, or which seem to manifest some discrepancy between their stated wishes and actual behaviour. Perhaps the easiest illustration is where an individual acknowledges that drug use is causing some difficulty, and commits to changing drug use as a result of this acknowledgement, yet finds that they continue to use the drugs in a similar or identical fashion. Many of those who smoke tobacco acknowledge that smoking is causing difficulties for them and threatens them with severe, long-term medical consequences, yet they continue to use tobacco. In seeking to address such a discrepancy, both the drug user and those observing the situation may employ a variety of explanatory/ descriptive models. Under such circumstances the drug user may be seen as being 'addicted', 'ill', 'weak', 'self-destructive', 'stubborn', 'perverted', or 'just plain stupid'.

The models used when discussing problems of 'addiction' are influenced by factors including empirical observation, philosophical assumptions, government policy and personal bias. Davies (1997) provides an excellent overview of the ways in which different attributional models are employed when articulating observations of those who use drugs.

Two fundamental assumptions seem important in considering how to account for some of the behaviours and experiences of drug-users: firstly, that there is a variety of possible explanatory and descriptive models available; and secondly, that each such model shapes the responses made to those who use drugs. For example, the view that drug use is a form of illness invites more medically-based 'treatments' than other models, whereas the view that drug use comprises some antisocial form of deviancy often invites more punitive and controlling responses.

The term 'dependency' has long been associated with those who use drugs and has often been used interchangeably with the term 'addiction'. For some the term 'drug dependency' may represent a useful way of thinking about the regularity with which an individual uses drugs, whereas for others it is viewed as a term that obscures efforts to understand the individual experience of particular drug-users.

Since the 1970s, 'dependency' has taken a more formal meaning, particularly in the context of medical diagnosis. Initially, attention was focused on the question of alcohol use: many influential bodies effected a shift from employing the term 'alcoholism' to thinking in terms of what was to become the 'alcohol dependence syndrome'. Subsequently there has been an upsurge in the tendency for researchers and theorists to employ concepts of dependence syndromes to drugs other than alcohol, including cannabis, heroin and nicotine. Accompanying this shift has been an invitation to separate concepts of 'dependency' and its harmful consequences. Although many might continue to argue that being dependent on a drug is a manifestation of harm, it is perhaps more helpful to accept that notions of dependency and harm are not synonymous. For example, it is easy to argue that most people are 'dependent on' motor vehicles, without at all having to argue that this is necessarily harmful.

Those who were initially responsible for positing the existence of 'dependency syndromes' felt that it was possible to offer the view that drug-users could be seen as occupying points on a continuum of dependency, ranging from zero or minimal dependency through to severe dependency. It was the intention of such authors to dispense with the tendency to ask *whether or not* someone was dependent, and to ask instead *how dependent* the individual might be upon a particular drug. In essence, it was argued that it is possible to observe changes in the psychobiological, subjective and behavioural spheres of an individual's life as a result of drug use. The more such changes were seen to be operating, the more 'dependent' the individual would be. The original proponents of the alcohol dependency syndrome (ADS) suggested that there were seven phenomena that could be quantified with a view to establishing at what point on the continuum of dependency a given individual might be placed at any particular time. The following description is taken from *DSM–IV* and is typical of similar criterion-based models:

Substance Dependence

A maladaptive pattern of substance use, leading to clinically significant impairment or distress, as manifested by three (or more) of the following, occurring at any time in the same twelve-month period:

(1) tolerance, as defined by either of the following:
   (a) a need for markedly increased amounts of the substance to achieve intoxication or desired effect.
   (b) markedly diminished effect with continued use of the same amount of the substance.

(2) withdrawal, as manifested by either of the following:
   (a) the characteristic withdrawal syndrome for the substance (refer to Criteria A and B of the criteria sets for withdrawal from the specific substances).
   (b) the same (or a closely related) substance is taken to relieve or avoid withdrawal symptoms.

(3) the substance is often taken in larger amounts or over a longer period than was intended.

(4) there is a persistent desire or unsuccessful efforts to cut down or control substance use.

(5) a great deal of time is spent in activities necessary to obtain the substance (e.g., visiting multiple doctors or driving long distances), use the substance (e.g., chain-smoking), or recover from its effects.

(6) important social, occupational, or recreational activities are given up or reduced because of substance use.

(7) the substance use is continued despite knowledge of having a persistent or recurrent physical or psychological problem that is likely to have been caused or exacerbated by the substance (e.g., current cocaine use despite recognition of cocaine-induced depression, or continued drinking despite recognition that an ulcer was made worse by alcohol consumption).

Specify if:

With physiological dependence: evidence of tolerance or withdrawal (i.e., either Item 1 or 2 is present)
Without physiological dependence: no evidence of tolerance or withdrawal (i.e., neither Item 1 nor 2 is present).

(American Psychiatric Association 1994)

The notion of dependency may have a useful function in providing a framework in which to think about some of the experiences encountered by those who use drugs regularly. However, such a construct also carries with it the risk of reification, i.e. the propensity to regard an abstract concept as having material validity. In the therapeutic situation, we are concerned to enter into the deeply personal world of our clients and to understand the particular meaning and significance of experiences for the particular individual with whom we happen to be working. A tendency to process the client's material within the framework of a model of dependency may obstruct attempts to construct understanding deriving from the particulars of the client's experience. Counsellors will be familiar with the tension between establishing a good knowledge base of theory and developing the ability to attune themselves to the nuances and particularities of experience for each individual client. For many, it is the appreciation of the highly personal aspects of the client's experience as they unfold within the helping relationship that comprises the very essence of the process of counselling.

We need to be able to understand the experiences of our clients 'from within', rather than assessing the degree to which they conform to diagnostic or other categories. As with other theoretical constructs, the notion of dependency should be used in the service of facilitating this personal contact rather than being employed in ways that confound it.

Bill Reading

* * *

2.5 What are the most commonly used drugs, and how do they affect those who use them?

The most commonly used drugs

The most commonly used drug in the UK is caffeine. This mild stimulant is found in tea, coffee, colas and other soft drinks and in many over-the-counter medicines.

Britain's 'favourite' drug, however, is alcohol. Over 90 per cent of the adult population use it at least occasionally. Alcohol consumption can be measured in 'units' of alcohol. Most alcoholic drinks contain about one unit in a standard single measure. A pint of normal strength beer contains two units. Recommended safe levels of alcohol consumption are no more than three units a day (21 units per week) for a man, and two units a day (14 units per week) for a woman. About 16 per cent of men and 6 per cent of women exceed these levels. A person is likely to develop some kind of alcohol-related problem if consumption is greater than 50 units a week for a man and 35 units a week for a woman: 4 per cent of men and 1 per cent of women exceed this level of consumption.

Nicotine is the next most commonly used drug. The proportion of cigarette smokers in the adult population has fallen from over 50 per cent of men and 40 per cent of women in the 1970s, to 29 per cent of men and 28 per cent of women today. People aged 20–34 years are most likely to smoke. About two fifths of men and one third of women in this age group smoke, compared with less than a fifth of adults aged 60 and over. There have been several health campaigns aimed at persuading people to give up smoking. In a survey conducted in 1996, two thirds of current smokers aged 16 and over said that they would like to stop smoking.

Tranquillizers and hypnotics are some of the most commonly prescribed drugs in medical practice. Because of concerns about their potential for abuse and dependence, doctors are now advised to use these drugs with caution and for short periods only. In spite of this, many people are dependent on these drugs. They are subject to abuse and, as well as being obtained through prescriptions, these drugs can be bought and sold illegally on the 'black market'.

For illegal drugs, figures on consumption are more difficult to obtain. The British Crime Survey, conducted every two years by the Home Office, includes questions asking respondents about their use of various drugs. In 1998, 31 per cent of adults aged 16–59 years reported having used illicit drugs at some time in the past. Prevalence of drug use differs among age groups, with 52 per cent of 16–24-year-olds having used illicit drugs, but only 28 per cent of 45–54-year-olds.

Current drug use is less common. Only 10 per cent of 16–59-year-olds reported drug use in the last year and only 6 per cent in the last month. In terms of age group, 30 per cent of 16–24-year-olds reported drug use within the last twelve months and 20 per cent in the past 30 days, compared to 3.1 per cent and 1.5 per cent respectively for 45–54-year-olds.

Cannabis is the most frequently reported drug of use, with 25 per cent of all adults and 44 per cent of 16–24-year-olds having ever used it. Only 5 per cent of all adults and 17 per cent of those aged 16–24 had used it within the last month.

For other drugs, the highest prevalence of use is in 16–24-year-olds, decreasing with age to very low levels in the over-45 age group. In the youngest age group, 39 per cent report ever having taken hallucinogens (3 per cent in the last month), 21 per cent had ever used amphetamines (5 per cent in the last month), 11 per cent had ever taken ecstasy (2 per cent in the last month) and 7 per cent had taken cocaine (1 per cent in the last month). Only 1 per cent of the population has ever used opiates, and the only age group in which current levels of usage are not negligible is the 16–24-year-olds, in which 0.9 per cent of males and 0.5 per cent of females have used it in the last month.

The effects of drugs

Alcohol

Alcohol is a depressant of nervous system activity and is taken for its relaxing properties and the social benefits of mild disinhibition. Even in small doses, it can lead to a loss of coordination. In higher concentrations in the body, it can lead to loss of emotional control, clumsiness, confusion and stupor. In overdose, it can lead to respiratory suppression and death. Excessive use over time can lead to a variety of physical illnesses, especially of the liver, pancreas, stomach and central nervous system. It may also be associated with cardiovascular disease (although moderate drinking may have a protective effect against heart attack), and cancers of the head, neck, gastro-intestinal system and lung. Psychologically, it commonly produces depression and anxiety. Rarely, alcohol-induced psychosis may occur.

Nicotine

Nicotine has some stimulant effects, but also seems to directly affect the 'reward' system of the brain – a natural system that reinforces certain behaviours by producing pleasure. This reinforcing accounts for the strong addictive properties of nicotine. The adverse effects of cigarette smoking arise mainly from long-term use, which can lead to disability and death from lung disease (bronchitis, emphysema and lung cancer) and cardiovascular disease (heart attack, stroke).

Cannabis

Cannabis comes in many different forms, all of which are derived from the hemp plant *Cannabis sativa*. It can be smoked or eaten. Cannabis has several potential medical effects as an analgesic, anticonvulsant and hypnotic; it has also been used to treat nausea and to stimulate appetite. When used recreationally, it produces relaxation, euphoria and some perceptual changes: for example, time may seem to pass very slowly. In overdose, hallucinations and paranoia may occur and thinking becomes confused and disorganized, but it does not cause respiratory depression, and no deaths have been reported from the use of cannabis alone. The long-term health effects of cannabis are not clear, but if smoked it is likely to lead to lung disease. Suppression of testosterone levels and of sperm counts in men, and menstrual disturbances and reduced fertility in women have been reported, as have an 'amotivational syndrome' and 'cannabis psychosis' in some heavy users.

Hallucinogens

The most used hallucinogen is lysergic acid diethylamide (LSD), which is described here. Other hallucinogens include some naturally occurring compounds such as 'magic mushrooms' and the Mexican peyote cactus, which contains mescalin. LSD itself was first synthesized in 1938 by a chemist called Hofmann. Several other synthetic compounds engender hallucinogenic activity, such as DMT (dimethyltryptamine), DMA (dimethoxyamphetamine) and DOM (dimethoxymethylamphetamine), also known as STP (standing for serenity, tranquillity and peace).

The effects of LSD are very variable, depending on the expectations of the subject and the setting in which it is consumed. Characteristically, there are changes in perception. Stationary objects may seem to move, change shape or ripple. The size or relative importance of objects may change and colours become more intense. Sometimes sounds are 'seen' or 'felt' and colours 'heard' in a strange crossing over of perceptions. Technically, these changes are illusions (perceptual changes in existing objects) rather than hallucinations (perceptions which occur without an external stimulus). True hallucinations only rarely occur. Along with these perceptual changes, strong emotions may occur, such as a sublime feeling of 'oneness' with the world or the cosmos. Sometimes feelings of anxiety, fear or terror may be experienced. Often the subject may be pre-occupied with these experiences or become so confused as to lose touch with reality. At such times the risk of accidents is high. The main adverse effect of LSD is the 'bad trip' – a temporary episode of overwhelming anxiety or panic that may last up to 24 hours. If consumption of LSD is repeated quickly, the effects of any subsequent doses are much less. Because of this, the use of LSD is never repeated frequently enough to induce physical dependence. It has been suggested that LSD may some-times precipitate psychotic illness, but there is no clear evidence for this.

Stimulants

Amphetamines and cocaine are both taken for their stimulant properties. Caffeine is a mild stimulant and, if taken in large quantities, can produce anxiety, palpitations, tremor, irritability, insomnia and headache.

Ephedrine is a drug found in many decongestant medicines and is occasionally abused for its stimulant effects.

Amphetamines produce stimulation of the nervous system. They are sometimes used to improve alertness and concentration or to delay sleep. Medicinally they have also been used as appetite suppressants. When taken to produce pleasurable feelings of stimulation or excitement, they can be swallowed, sniffed or injected, either under the skin or into a vein. These latter methods result in a more rapid rise of concentration of the drug in the bloodstream producing a more rapid and intense effect, or 'high'. Overdosage or excessive use can lead to anxiety, agitation, irritability (possibly resulting in violence) and hypertension (which may lead to sub-arachnoid haemorrhage or stroke). Convulsions, coma or death may occur. Prolonged use may lead to a psychosis with auditory hallucinations and paranoid delusions.

The effects of cocaine are similar to amphetamines, but are more intense and shorter lived. There is an immediate intense effect or 'rush', followed by less intense stimulation that lasts for 30 minutes or so, often with a rebound effect of anxiety, depression and irritability. Cocaine can be swallowed, but is usually injected, sniffed or smoked. Cocaine can be processed to produce freebase or 'crack' cocaine, which produces an even more rapid effect when smoked. Repeated use of cocaine can produce auditory, visual or tactile hallucinations, including a sensation like insects crawling on the skin (formication) and paranoid psychosis. Sudden death may occur, either from convulsions and respiratory failure, or from cardiovascular events (heart attack, stroke). Sniffing of cocaine may lead to nasal discharge or to perforation of the nasal septum. Injection may lead to local ulceration of the skin, or to the transmission of blood-borne infections such as HIV or hepatitis.

Designer drugs

It is not difficult to make small chemical modifications to existing drugs resulting in new chemical compounds with similar properties to the parent drug. Sometimes this is done to alter the effects of the drug; sometimes a more potent compound can be produced; and sometimes it is simply a ploy to avoid drug regulations by producing new substances that are not covered by existing laws. Modifications of stimulants, hallucinogens and opiates have been produced. Perhaps the best known of these drugs is ecstasy, or MDMA (3, 4, methylene-dioxymethamphetamine), a compound that has stimulant and mild hallucinogenic properties. It has been particularly associated with raves – all night parties in which participants dance energetically to continuous repetitive rhythmic music. In this setting, deaths have occurred with ecstasy due to raised body temperature, dehydration and eventual circulatory collapse.

Sedatives

As long as medicine has been practised, tranquillizers and sedatives have been given to relieve distress and suffering and to promote sleep. In modern times it has become common practice to 'treat' many forms of emotional distress, including normal emotional reactions, such as bereavement, with such compounds. In the past barbiturates were commonly prescribed, but these were recognized to promote physical dependence. They are also very dangerous in overdose because they depress respiration. When the benzodiazepines were invented, they were widely used because they are much safer in overdose and were originally thought not to be addictive. Well-known drugs of this type include the tranquillizers diazepam (Valium) and chlordiazepoxide (Librium) and the sleeping tablets temazepam and nitrazepam (Mogadon). Although these drugs are relatively free from adverse physical effects, it is now known that they do cause addiction, with quite rapid development of tolerance and withdrawal symptoms. The main adverse effect is on concentration, and they should not be used when someone needs to drive or operate machinery because of the risk of accidents. Their use should now be restricted to carefully selected patients for short periods only; and wherever possible non-drug treatments, such as counselling, and emotional support should be used for most emotional problems.

Opiates

Although opiates are not widely used, it is probably the user of opiates who first comes to mind when we think of 'drug abuse' or 'drug dependence'. Certainly, much of the drugs policy in Britain and most of the addiction services are targeted towards this group of drug users. There is a wide variety of opiates, either derived from the naturally occurring compounds in the opium poppy or manufactured synthetically. Opium itself is a mixture of alkaloids, including morphine and codeine, derived directly from the opium poppy. Morphine is a naturally occurring compound, and heroin (diamorphine) is derived from it by a simple chemical process. Methadone is a synthetic opiate analgesic with a long duration of action. Pethidine and dipipanone (Diconal) are just two amongst many synthetic opiates.

All of the opiates have similar effects, the main differences being in their potency and duration of action. Firstly, they are powerful analgesics. Because of this property, they have been of inestimable benefit to mankind as a whole. They remain some of the most effective and widely used therapeutic agents available today. In addition to the direct analgesic effect, they also induce euphoria, a state of mental detachment and wellbeing, and have a sedative effect, with impairment of concentration, drowsiness and sleep. Overdose may cause unconsciousness, respiratory depression and death. Other effects may include nausea, constricted (pin-point) pupils, suppression of cough and constipation. Opiates may be smoked, inhaled (i.e. 'snorted'), taken orally or injected. The most widely abused opiate is heroin, probably because it is more likely to produce euphoria and less likely to promote nausea or vomiting than other opiates. It may be taken orally or by intramuscular or subcutaneous injection, but is most often taken by intravenous injection (mainlining), or by 'chasing the dragon' – heating the heroin on a piece of foil and inhaling the fumes. Apart from the risk of death by overdose, many of the health risks of opiate use derive from injections, especially if syringes or needles are shared amongst users. There is a high risk of blood-borne diseases, such as HIV and hepatitis B or C. Intravenous injection may also result in abscesses at the injection site, accidental injection into an artery or septicaemia.

Solvents

Volatile solvents, which are used to keep adhesives in a fluid state, are sometimes inhaled for their intoxicating effects. These substances are found in glues, lighter and other gas fuels, paint thinners, aerosol sprays and even in Tippex correcting fluid. Inhalation leads to intoxication, with changes in mood, lack of judgement and disinhibition. Usually this takes place in groups of youngsters in their early and middle teens. Most will 'grow out of it', but for a few the habit continues and is then pursued alone. The main danger is death from the toxic effects of the fumes or from accidents whilst intoxicated. There have been some cases where death has occurred as a result of paralysis of the larynx, in situations where aerosols have been sprayed directly into the throat. There are also some rare but very serious organic consequences, including various neurological disorders and liver or kidney damage.

Bill Plummer

* * *

2.6 Is all drug use harmful?

The short answer to this question is 'No'!

However, simply to say this is to miss an opportunity to examine what we mean by harm, the factors that contribute to it, how we evaluate the harms caused by different substances, and some of the principles under-pinning efforts to reduce them. Any drug can be used without harm – including those that are most demonized within society such as heroin and crack cocaine. Nevertheless, all drugs (meaning legal and illegal substances) carry a risk of harm, including those that society tolerates, notably nicotine, alcohol and caffeine. Any drug can be used without harm yet no drug is without risk. Furthermore, this question is an evalua-tive one, which appears to focus only on the 'costs' of drug use. It some-times seems there is a taboo on any acknowledgement of the benefits of drug use, yet these are why some people tend to use them, and this must be considered in addressing the question.

Harm is in part a socially constructed concept, not a fixed property of any given drug. Additionally, harm – and its avoidance – is shaped massively by the context in which use occurs. In the early nineteenth century, the many agricultural opium eaters in East Anglia buying their opium at the local 'druggists' would largely have regarded their opium use as entirely ordinary and unproblematic. There was little or no discus-sion of a Fenland 'opium problem'. It was available, more or less afford-able and highly functional for people, many of them working in gruelling conditions draining the fens (see Berridge 1999, for a detailed account of this little known feature of Victorian values). In contrast, because of its propensity to cause harm by stimulating rebellious thought, Charles II attempted to suppress London's coffee houses in 1675, less than 50 years after the vizier of Constantinople attempted something similar by round-ing up coffee-house customers and having them sewn into bags and thrown in the river (Walton 2001; Weinberg and Bealer 2001). Yet today this answer can be typed by an author fuelled on endless, legally acquired supplies of *Coffea arabica*! More recently, between the 1970s and the 1990s, ecstasy moved from being seen as an esoteric but benign pharmaceutical, with some applications as an adjunct to psychotherapy, to a pariah drug likely to result in its users ending up unconscious and intubated in a hospital bed or worse. The way we perceive the harm that drugs cause is not fixed, but shaped by empirical facts, politics and the media.

Researchers help shape our understanding of harm by generating empirical evidence of its nature, cause and extent within populations. But the media and wider political processes shape our understanding of harm by their control of what we are told, the way we are told it, what research gets funded and what knowledge is therefore generated. Thus, although the number of people who die annually of alcohol overdose is broadly equivalent to the number dying after taking ecstasy, deaths from 'alcohol poisoning' do not attract the same coverage as those from ecstasy. As early epidemiology progressively revealed the risks of opium overdose during the nineteenth century, this contributed to the pressure to change the way its availability was regulated. Similarly, whereas HIV has resulted in a phenomenal, global research programme, the more prevalent hepatitis C, which affects about 30 per cent of English drug injectors, has received comparatively little attention. And whereas some drugs such as tobacco are advertised – most strikingly in the present targeting of new markets in developing countries – others, such as cannabis, are prohibited as a result of international law.

The societal treatment of different drugs also directly shapes the harms that result. Alcohol prohibition in America led to a boom in its illegal manufacture, which sometimes resulted in the accidental supply of highly toxic methanol instead of our preferred alcohol – ethanol. Similarly, the criminalized nature of heroin supply makes it harder for people to be certain of the dose and contents of what they are using, and discourages the promotion of injecting hygiene that in turn prevents infection with various bacteria and blood-borne viruses. The regulatory framework for drug supply (or their prohibition) is one of the key contextual factors shaping the harm that results.

If my example of coffee seems flippant, it is worth bearing in mind that the LD50 (lethal dose for 50 per cent of the adult population) of caffeine is just 10 grams, or less than half an ounce. The way caffeine is generally available within society makes it unlikely that people will use this much, which is the equivalent of about 100 espressos in one sitting; and arguably the intoxication that this would induce is not especially sought after.

In contrast, the LD50 for heroin or cocaine is rather closer to the dose that many people would choose in order to feel the effects of the intoxication that these drugs produce. An allied point to this is that harm (and pleasure) often increases when the use of a drug moves from a natural form to a refined version. Using refined drugs commonly allows a more intense experience, making a drug more alluring, and increasing the ease with which overdose can occur. However, one only has to think of the hazards of obtaining natural highs derived from *Datura* and *Fly agaric* to appreciate that simple equations such as 'natural = safe', or 'refined = dangerous', should be resisted.

Frequently, unrefined drugs have been accommodated within cultures over a period of centuries or millennia in a way that also allows a number of cultural controls to evolve and reduce harm. Restricting use to sacramental purposes or limiting use to certain rites of passage are two ways in which this occurs. Contemporary examples include simpler 'rules' such as not having a drink until 'the sun is over the yard arm', and the increased disapproval of drink-driving. It may be helpful to think of turn-of-the-century English society as being in the same process of accommodation to refined drugs such as heroin, cocaine and ecstasy. Experience with alcohol as a result of the colonial exploits of different European countries graphically illustrates how introducing a new drug into populations which lack these controls, as in Aboriginal Australia, can result in quite devastating patterns of drug use. It is similarly striking how efforts to control harm from traditional drugs – notably opium and coca – can result in increased harm when populations turn to refined drugs where traditional crops are less accessible.

The idea of harm-free heroin use may also seem questionable to some. However, diamorphine (heroin) use in medical settings is a long-established and effective practice for pain control. When administered properly, even long-term use is not known to cause harm beyond the risk of dependence: which is itself only harmful when you want to stop or have none of the drug available. Even when we examine heroin use and dependence, we find that things are far from the way we might assume. This is most evident within research among 470 US soldiers returning from Vietnam (Robins 1974). Heroin use was very high among soldiers in Vietnam. During 1971, approaching half (44 per cent) of all soldiers reported trying one or more 'narcotic' opiate drugs (mostly heroin or opium) during their tour of duty, and a fifth considered themselves to 'have been addicted'. However, on follow-up in the USA between eight and twelve months after their return only 9.5 per cent reported having used any 'narcotic' since their return, and only 7 per cent considered that they were 'addicted'.

The most important development in recent years has been the evolution of the 'Harm Reduction' movement. When thinking about harm, its theorists generally consider different 'types' and different 'levels', as Newcombe's classification shows in Table 2.1. 'Health' consequences include the physical and psychological results of drug use; 'social' refers to factors such as aggression or other antisocial behaviour in public

spaces; and 'economic' consequences include the burden to society arising from drug-related crime, costs to our health and criminal justice
systems and the revenue from regulated drugs such as alcohol and
tobacco. The 'level' categories concern the 'individual' drug user, their
immediate family, friends, neighbours or work colleagues ('community'),
and the 'societal' level, which includes factors such as effects on civil
rights, or the general angst about 'the drugs problem' within society in
general.

Table 2.1. (From Newcombe 1992)

Level	Type		
	Health	*Social*	*Economic*
Individual			
Community			
Societal			

Harm reduction typically concentrates on the negative consequences of
drug use and broadly uses a cost/benefit type of calculus to evaluate the
case for intervention. As a philosophy firmly grounded in public health its
emphasis is preventive, and it attempts to takes account of long-term
consequences such as the incidence of liver cancer among people infected
with hepatitis C – an outcome that may arise 25 years after the original
infection.

Recently a limitation has become evident in the lack of any theoretical
basis for determining how conflicts between different objectives can be
resolved. Since 1997 there has been a marked shift in national policy
away from a pre-eminent concern with the health of individual drug
users, and towards one that attaches greater importance to community
and societal harms and crime prevention (Stimson 2000). Decisions as to
what types of harm we focus upon are essentially value-based political
decisions, and cannot be resolved by appeal to any particular theoretical
guidance. However, harm reductionists generally work from the view
that, as in any other realm of health and social care, interventions with
drug users should primarily be driven by concern for the wellbeing of the
individual drug user; and that other concerns, though important, are
subordinate.

In seeking to reduce drug-related harm some established principles from the 'harm reduction' movement that should underpin any interventions include:

- empowering people with accurate information
- working within a hierarchy of types of harm towards goals that are achievable for the drug user
- treating drug users with the same respect and dignity that any other user of health and social care services might expect
- basing intervention on the best available scientific evidence
- making services accessible
- offering a range of options that are consistent with the needs of the drug user rather than the therapeutic preferences of the service or its practitioners.

Finally, the beneficial consequences of drug use cannot be ignored, although factoring them into any form of rational cost–benefit analysis will never be possible, because of the value-judgements that bedevil such a project. For obvious reasons research into the benefits of drug use receives little government funding, though some of the benefits that are commonly claimed include:

- increased creativity
- relaxation
- social 'lubrication'
- enhancing spirituality
- increased personal awareness and enhancing interactions between people
- providing pleasure or euphoria
- improved productivity through increased alertness or use as a self-reward scheme
- providing some capacity to cope with emotional problems.

Only the individual can determine whether the delights of a blast from crack cocaine, the mystical insight from ayahuasca, a cannabis-induced daze, the euphoric oblivion of heroin use or the glow from ecstasy are worth the risk of harm that accompanies them. In dealing with drug use and drug users we should always remember this.

Neil Hunt

* * *

2.7 What are withdrawal symptoms? And do they happen with all drugs?

The human body has an amazing capacity to adapt to changing circumstances and demands. One example of this is the way in which the body adapts to repeated drug or alcohol use over time. If a drug produces pleasurable experiences and its use is repeated, frequently the systems of the body will adapt to minimize the effects of its continuing presence. It is as if the body were trying to 'resume normal functioning' in spite of the drug and its effects. The systems that remove the drug from the body, through metabolism or excretion, become more active. Many drugs are metabolized (inactivated or broken down) by proteins in the liver called enzymes. The amount of these enzymes may increase. For example, with alcohol, the enzyme gamma glutamyl transferase (gamma GT) increases quite dramatically, and this can be used as a simple blood test for excessive alcohol consumption (as the amount of enzyme in the blood also increases).

The effects of drugs on the nervous system are minimized by changes in the nerve cells, especially in the systems of chemical messengers or 'transmitters', which carry information from one nerve cell to the next. The production or breakdown of these transmitters may increase or diminish and the number of receptors that bind with them may also change. There may also be changes in the number and type of connections between nerve cells in different nerve pathways in the brain.

These changes may take many weeks, months or even years of continued drug use to develop, and although some of them can be reversed quite quickly if drug use is suddenly stopped, other changes may take longer to reverse, or may even be permanent.

Over a period of time, therefore, the body (particularly the nervous system) becomes adapted to the presence of the drug within the body. In effect, the systems of the body will only work properly if the drug is present. If consumption of the drug is then suddenly stopped the nervous system will not function properly and symptoms of varying severity may occur. This could perhaps be likened to a tug of war in which one team (the body) is pulling harder and harder against another team (the effects of the drug), which then suddenly and unexpectedly lets go!

Features of this kind of adaptation are *tolerance*, in which the person needs to consume larger amounts of the drug to obtain the same effect; *withdrawal symptoms*, which occur if the drug is stopped suddenly; and *frequent* use of the drug in order to prevent withdrawal symptoms. It is possible that *cravings* for the drug may include a physical mechanism related to bodily adaptation, although many other factors also determine whether cravings occur. The *rapid re-institution* of heavy drug use after a period of abstinence may also be a sign of adaptation, although this too is influenced by many other factors, including personal and social expectations.

When the body becomes adapted to the presence of a drug in this way, the changes in the nervous system are known as 'neuro-adaptation' and the overall picture is often described as 'physical dependence'. This term is not entirely satisfactory. Although the body depends on the continued use of the drug in order to avoid withdrawal symptoms, this does not mean that the continued health or wellbeing of the person depends on continuing use of the drug. If the drug is stopped, the body will sooner or later adapt to its absence, just as it adapted to its presence in the first place.

Not all drugs produce this kind of adaptation. Those that are most likely to do so are the sedative or tranquillizing drugs, including alcohol, and the opiates. With sedatives, and particularly with alcohol, withdrawal symptoms may be very serious, even life threatening. Withdrawal from opiates can also be very unpleasant, but is not usually dangerous or life threatening.

However, it should be noted that even with these drugs not everybody will suffer from withdrawal symptoms, and of those who do only a proportion will have symptoms of such severity that they require medication. Only a very small number will have such serious symptoms that they require hospital admission for treatment.

Specific symptoms of withdrawal with *alcohol and other sedatives* include anxiety, restlessness, agitation, insomnia, tremor, palpitations, flushing, sweating and gastro-intestinal symptoms, such as nausea, vomiting and diarrhoea. Muscle weakness and loss of coordination, muscular pains and headache may occur. Concentration and memory may be impaired. Fatigue and depression may occur, as may panic attacks or phobic anxiety. With alcohol, more severe symptoms include confusion and disorientation. Illusions and visual or auditory hallucinations and/or paranoid delusions may occur. This may result in the full-blown syndrome of delirium tremens, with severe agitation and confusion, terrifying hallucinations and severe paranoid anxiety. With both sedatives and alcohol, epileptic convulsions may occur on sudden withdrawal.

With *opiates*, withdrawal symptoms include lassitude, anxiety, restlessness, insomnia and depression. There is increased flow of saliva, nasal secretions and tears, and vomiting and diarrhoea may occur. Pains occur in the muscles and joints and there is abdominal cramping. Specific features include frequent yawning, dilated pupils and a gooseflesh appearance to the skin, which gives rise to the term 'cold turkey'. The onset and duration of symptoms depend on the half-life of the drug – a measure of its duration of action within the body.

With *stimulants*, some tolerance develops if the drugs are used frequently. Sudden withdrawal after heavy usage may result in a mixture of the kind of withdrawal symptoms described for sedatives, together with lassitude, sleepiness and depression. Sometimes depression is so severe that there may be a risk of suicide.

The severity of withdrawal symptoms, and the ability of an individual to cope with them, depend to a large extent on the expectations of the person, the social setting and the degree of emotional and practical support which they are able to access. Sometimes a person makes repeated attempts to withdraw, but does not manage to remain abstinent until the withdrawal symptoms have passed their peak and begun to subside. This may lead to feelings of failure, hopelessness and helplessness, and a fear that the withdrawal symptoms are unbounded or unbearable.

Sometimes, support, reassurance and practical help are all that are needed to help a person in withdrawal from drugs or alcohol. Sometimes medication is helpful. The main reason for using medication is to prevent serious medical complications. It may also reduce withdrawal symptoms, but it is unlikely to abolish them completely. For alcohol, medical treatment is usually with benzodiazepines, such as diazepam. These do not usually need to be continued for more than a few days. For benzodiazepine withdrawal, the dose can be reduced over a period of two to several weeks, usually after switching to a longer-acting drug, whose levels in the body fall relatively slowly.

For opiates, the symptoms of withdrawal can be treated by drugs such as clonidine or lofexidine. Acupuncture has also been used with some success. Alternatively, the opiate can be replaced by methadone, a long-acting opiate, and this can then be reduced and stopped over the course of a few weeks.

Bill Plummer

* * *

2.8 Is it true that some people keep craving for drugs even after they have stopped using them for long periods? Is this what is meant by the term 'psychological dependence'?

The notions of 'craving' and 'psychological dependence' have been ubiquitous in the field of substance misuse for many years. Whilst their use emerged initially as descriptions that attempted to capture the experience, increasingly the terms evolved into clinical markers, which formed part of an overall diagnosis such as 'alcoholic', 'alcohol/drug dependent', etc. In this context the perceived presence of craving and dependence served and still serves to distinguish 'normal' substance use from 'abnormal', and 'pathological' from 'non-pathological'. Whilst in a scientific sense these ideas are greatly challenged and largely unsustainable, in both popular usage and many treatment settings the construct of what Davies (2000) refers to as 'addiction-as-disease' remains dominant, purely because in his view it is a highly functional perception. (For further discussion of these and related issues see Questions 2.2, 2.3 and 2.4.)

What is 'craving'?

The general dictionary definition of craving as 'a strong desire' does not completely fit the definition of craving as applied to substance misuse. It has been noted (Drummond 2000) that clients, clinicians and researchers use the term interchangeably to describe a host of experiences including desire, urge, liking, wanting, needing, compulsion, intending, wishing and the like. The only unifying factor is that these all refer to the anticipated use of a substance. In general, he concludes, craving can be functionally defined as 'the conscious experience of a desire to take a drug'. It becomes immediately apparent that this definition is equally applicable to non-problematic, everyday substance use.

Theoretical models of craving have been classified into three main categories:

1. Phenomenological models – based on clinical observations, practical experience, interview and interaction with that section of the population identified as misusing substances.
2. Conditioning models – based on conditioning theory that postulates craving as a conditioned symptom of withdrawal from a substance,

which persists long after the withdrawal phase; that is, a stimulus such as the sight of alcohol can trigger this conditioned response, part of which is the experience of craving.

3. Cognitive theories – these are grounded in social learning theory and relate to belief, attribution, self-efficacy and the interplay with behavioural conditioning.

In summary, Beck et al. (1993) describe four main types of craving in process terms.

1. Craving in response to withdrawal symptoms – the need to 'feel better again'
2. Response to lack of pleasure – trying to improve mood
3. Conditioned response to drug cues – as described under conditioning models
4. Hedonistic desires – the use of drugs to enhance another experience, playing music and smoking cannabis for example.

What is psychological dependence?

As with the term craving, definitions seek to posit psychological dependence as a discrete entity. Russell (1976) makes a distinction between dependent and non-dependent by focusing on the 'crucial feature of negative affect in the absence (or anticipated absence) of the drug'.

Two related processes describe the 'acquisition' of psychological dependence:

1. A learned behaviour that has been shaped by a host of reinforcers related to the biological factors of increased tolerance to a substance, which in turn perpetuates increased amounts used and precipitates withdrawal in its absence.
2. Substances may be used to aid intrapersonal and interpersonal functioning. For example, to relax, forget, give confidence, disinhibit, sleep and the like. Eventually, it becomes difficult to manage these situations without the associated substance use and its absence, or possible absence, becomes a source of anxiety.

This is just a brief exploration of these theoretical constructs, and as Edwards et al. (1997) note, further insights into these phenomena involve advances in understanding the relevant biological, behavioural and cognitive processes and their subsequent interactions.

The therapeutic context

Within the context of counselling and therapy, the notions of choice, free-dom and personal responsibility are of course central. This may be at odds with models that present craving and psychological dependence as experiences that do not allow the person to act autonomously. The impli-cation is, as Davies (2000) puts it, that 'the person in question does not simply want, but in some sense has to have something'. It is vital, there-fore, that the clinical definition of concepts such as craving and psycho-logical dependence are given personal meaning through the client's verbalized experience, so that a shared understanding can be arrived at. Whilst it is incumbent upon the counsellor or therapist to foster the necessary environment to facilitate this type of exploration, it can be a very difficult process, as clients are often effectively socialized into labelling their experiences, and may need to 'unlearn' this language if it inhibits understanding. Some time ago several clients in a group setting were routinely referring to their 'cravings' for alcohol. Each member was asked in turn to define their cravings for themselves. Without exception, each produced a deeply personal statement imbued with feelings that illustrated the nature and significance of their relationship with alcohol. Statements such as 'a thirst only alcohol can quench', 'wishing for that special glow', and 'time for a holiday from reality' captured the essence of what the absence of alcohol might mean.

Once a client's experience is 'de-labelled' and worked with creatively, ideas of craving and psychological dependence no longer function as discrete entities, but become amenable to normal contextual exploration. This is invariably both instructive and productive as the emotional and environmental setting of these experiences emerges. A thought or feeling, which has consistently been responded to by using a substance, might eventually be extinguished, and in time be recognized and experienced only as a craving. In this sense, a craving is also a marker: a covert or disguised expression of a more complex, generic set of personal thoughts and feelings. As Jackson (1997) observes, 'If allowed, when talking about cravings, clients will often associate to what for them are difficult feeling states such as sadness, anxiety and depression.' Furthermore, it is likely that these personal areas are not solely the product of the client's substance use, but also figure significantly in their overall reasons for orig-inally using drugs and/or alcohol.

It also becomes apparent that clients' subjective experiences of craving are not static, but rather are greatly influenced by their situational factors, and perhaps more importantly by how they perceive themselves, both generally and within these situations. We know that it is likely that certain cues will prompt certain responses, such as a client having been abstinent for a week experiencing strong cravings upon entering his old pub. Equally, more personal attributes related to efficacy and decision-making play a significant part, and clinical observation often suggests that craving only exists in the context of possible gratification. Therefore, clients often feel untroubled by cravings in situations where they might normally be expected to experience them, if they have made a personally irrevocable decision not to use substances at that time.

Two examples illustrate this process. Firstly, clients who have established a pattern of drinking every few months are often completely untroubled by thoughts of alcohol during their 'dry times'. Paradoxically, the certainty of drinking again perhaps allows considerable, enjoyable periods of abstinence to be established. Secondly, clients who elect to take Antabuse, a substance that produces a powerfully unpleasant physical response if alcohol is taken (see Question 6.10), often describe being liberated from thoughts of drinking, apparently because they feel they could not, even if they wanted to.

Further, as with all presenting problems, the client's personal sense of esteem, efficacy and ability to respond to his/her difficulties influence the experience itself. Viewed purely from a behavioural perspective, cravings that are not reinforced through using drink/drugs will eventually be extinguished. These approaches are particularly relevant to Relapse Prevention models (see particularly Questions 5.5, 5.6 and 5.7).

Exploring these terms with a client is essentially based on the use of good counselling skills within the context of a healthy therapeutic relationship. This is no different from the way the counsellor might explore any term a client may use, in that personal meaning and significance need to be clarified, because experience cannot be separated from the person. However, counsellors need to feel secure enough in their own roles to facilitate this process, particularly as some clients may be reluctant initially to look beyond technical terms, which can be used defensively against looking at the more personal aspects. It may be easier for some clients to attribute their drug use to their 'cravings' or 'psychological dependence' because this externalizes the problem, and can serve as a way of distancing the therapist. And while counsellors will of course work sensitively in these areas, they equally need to establish their own models of understanding, so as to inform their interventions.

Paul Jackson

CHAPTER 3

Drug and alcohol problems in general counselling practice

3.1 Are there ways in which I might be able to tell if a client has a problem with drink or drugs?

Ideally, the generic counsellor will incorporate at least a brief exploration of the client's substance use within the assessment process. There are two main reasons for this. Firstly, to ascertain whether the client's substance use has any part to play in his or her presenting difficulties. Secondly, and leading on from this, whether any substance use will impinge upon the client's ability to fully engage in the therapeutic relationship.

Counsellor resistance

Before looking at how the counsellor might identify whether the client has a problem with drink or drugs, it is important to discuss reasons as to why the counsellor may at times not wish to undertake this exploration. Broadly, these can be described in terms of, firstly, the counsellor's role and, secondly, the beliefs, attitudes and 'person' of the counsellor.

Counsellor role

The counsellor may not feel it is a legitimate issue to raise in the first instance: 'Is the client's use of drink/drugs any of my business?'

Counsellors may feel that they do not have the skills to respond usefully to any potential substance misuse problem the client may have: 'It's safer not to ask.'

The counsellor may not have the factual knowledge relating to signs, symptoms and effects of drink/drug misuse: 'I don't know what I'm looking for anyway.'

41

An enquiry of this sort may be at odds with the counsellor's personal model and approach, or the overall agency policy/philosophy: 'It's not what I/we do.'

The person of the counsellor

Macdonald and Patterson (1991) suggest that drug-users in particular elicit stereotypical attitudinal responses in counsellors and wider society alike, whereby the client subsequently becomes caricatured, and the person is seen as the problem:

- moral – the client is seen as weak, worthless, depraved
- legal – the client is seen as bad or wicked
- medical – the client is seen as sick or ill
- social and political – the client is seen as a victim of the social or political environment.

Broadly, these observations are also manifest in the response to those with alcohol problems.

The counsellor's motivation and ability to explore a client's substance use will be greatly influenced by his or her own use of drink and drugs. For example, counsellors who use cannabis recreationally themselves are likely to view the client's use of the same substance differently from a counsellor who leads a drug-free lifestyle. These tend to be thorny issues and promote a lot of defensiveness on the part of the counsellor, which again is likely to affect the nature and content of the counselling relationship.

As with any enquiry, it is important that the counsellor strives to maintain the integrity of the relationship and remains empathic to the client's current position. It is helpful for counsellors to give some thought as to how they will ask about the client's substance use. They may simply ask directly – 'Could you tell me about your current use of drink and drugs?' – or they may ask about drink and drugs separately. If this direct enquiry is made, then it is helpful to explain the purpose behind it and to avoid asking in a flat, cursory way that might give the impression of getting something awkward out the way. Equally, the counsellor may delay any enquiry until it can be related directly to what the client is addressing at the time. This way is often more engaging and facilitative, but necessitates the counsellor tolerating the anxiety that a suitable intervention point may not emerge.

If the client does begin to talk about their drink and drug use, it is important that the counsellor continues to explore this in the context of their life in the here-and-now, rather than becoming preoccupied with whether the client is 'addicted', an 'alcoholic', etc. This type of enquiry is likely to engender defensiveness in clients, particularly if they begin to feel that the counsellor is more interested in gathering information than in relating to them. As always, the relationship must be preserved; the issue of the client's substance use can always be returned to.

Indications of possible drug or alcohol misuse

These can be divided into two main categories: firstly, those that are observable; secondly, those that emerge out of the dialogue between client and counsellor.

Observable indicators

Intoxication during the sessions is probably obvious in the case of alcohol since the client is likely to smell strongly of drink and behave in ways that suggest intoxication. However, it may be less obvious with the heavy-drinking client who has developed an increased tolerance to alcohol and can function seemingly appropriately having consumed large amounts. Even so, some disinhibiting factors are likely to be present.

Generally, the situation with drugs is less clear-cut, and observable factors less obvious, particularly as different drug use obviously produces different effects. The counsellor might note fluctuating levels of consciousness, labile presentation that does not seem contextually correct, rapid and excitable speech content, inability to settle, etc. Whilst it may seem a daunting task, it is important that the counsellor establishes at least a working knowledge of the effects of both alcohol and drugs.

Withdrawal during the sessions: the client presenting in acute withdrawal is likely to be obvious to the counsellor, not least because he or she will be in some distress or discomfort, even if this has become a regular occurrence. Withdrawal at less acute levels is not so apparent and may present as more generalized anxiety or panic experiences. (For further information, see Question 2.7.)

Physical appearance: this is quite difficult to describe as clients obviously present routinely in very different ways. Because a client presents as unkempt, red-faced and flushed may or may not be significant in the context of possible alcohol and drug misuse, but is perhaps worthy of note. Less ambiguous is the presence of scars or wounds around injection sites in intravenous drug use.

Process indicators

How often does the client make reference to his or her alcohol and drug use within the session? The client may regularly describe how much they 'enjoy a drink', situations where they frequently get drunk, or make reference to the process of their drinking, such as 'I don't enjoy a quiet drink, I drink to get drunk'. They may make ambiguous references, along the lines of 'I need a drink to get me going'. Alternatively, the client may describe smoking cannabis nightly as the 'only way of unwinding'. In general, clients tend to refer more readily to their use of alcohol, cannabis, and psychotropic medication such as diazepam, but may be more reticent to disclose details of their other drug use, most obviously due to concerns over the legal implications. Equally, the client may appear to studiously avoid any reference to alcohol and drugs.

Alternatively, any statements may be accompanied by rationalizations around their use, defensive comments or expressions of anger or irritation with the counsellor:

> Yes I do drink regularly, but don't we all?
> Of course I like a drink, but I can take it or leave it.
> Listen, if your job was as stressful as mine, you'd smoke dope every night.
> Why are you so interested in whether I take drugs, are you the police or something?
> Are you telling me you don't have a little something to relax after listening to us lot all day?

Clients will often describe managing some of their presenting difficulties with drink or drugs, effectively 'self-medicating'. A client may reduce anxiety by steadily using cannabis throughout the day, or cope with bouts of depression, for example, by drinking heavily.

The client may make reference in passing to alcohol or drug-related consequences, but not elaborate further: 'My partner said I was spending too much on cannabis'; ' I've been warned twice at work for smelling of drink in the morning', etc. There may be references to alcohol/drug misuse problems in the past. Whilst not necessarily indicating a current problem, it is nevertheless appropriate to ascertain current use in view of this information.

Although it may be more convenient when the client openly acknowledges any difficulties with alcohol and drugs during the assessment process, in practice this often emerges over a number of sessions. In some ways this is helpful for the counsellor, as counsellor and client have hopefully been able to establish a stronger relationship, which itself may have prompted the client's disclosure. Additionally, the counsellor will have sense enough of the client to judge their normal mode of functioning, presentation, etc., which will help in identifying those times when they may be affected by the use of drink or drugs.

Velleman (1992) has stated, in words that are equally applicable to both drink and drugs: 'In all assessments it is worth having the question "Is there an alcohol-related difficulty here?" in our minds. If we avoid addressing the question, it will probably get in the way of all our other work.'

Paul Jackson

* * *

3.2 Are there ways in which a counsellor may be able to help the client recognize that drink or drugs may be a problem?

Of paramount importance in addressing this question is the centrality of the therapeutic relationship. Whilst in any therapeutic endeavour this is always the case, particularly as the relationship itself is increasingly now being understood as the agent of change, it becomes even more central when starting to address issues that may engender profound ambivalence in the client. The counsellor, therefore, needs to cultivate an ambience of mutual openness, trust and honesty – the experience of being together in an endeavour that can be conceptualized as the therapeutic alliance. While different counsellors will foster this relationship in the context of their personal model and philosophy, from the perspective of drug and alcohol agencies this stage in the process is a time at which counsellors are likely to be very active in attempting to promote a facilitative environment for the client. Therefore the suggestions made here all need to be considered in the light of this evolving relationship, rather than as practical ideas in isolation.

Facilitating openness

(i)   Attend to the quality of the relationship, as stated above.

(ii) It is important that the counsellor remains sensitive to the client's pace, both in terms of how the client works on himself or herself generally, and more specifically in respect of any drug or alcohol-related issues.

(iii) However well intentioned, it is vital that the counsellor does not attempt to 'enlighten' the client with what may seem to be obvious evidence of a drink/drug problem. Counsellors do not normally respond this way to other issues in the client's life; this type of intervention only promotes defensiveness.

(iv) Linked to the above, the counsellor needs to consider how any intervention may be integrated into his or her individual style. Whilst this is obviously allied to the counsellor's model and philosophy, it is much more about the practicalities of how the counsellor is 'present' with the client. This integration requires considerable thought from the counsellor. For example, it may be difficult for a very analytically oriented counsellor to be more obviously active in the session and ask specific questions about this aspect of the client's life, particularly if a defined mode of inactivity has been the norm.

If these considerations are avoided, then the counsellor's personal discomfort increases the likelihood of also avoiding any possibly problematic drink and drug use by the client.

Facilitative interventions

Assuming that there is reason to believe a client may have problems related to drink and drug use and the client may at least be able to consider this possibility, then the following ways can help the counsellor facilitate this recognition:

(i) In all these interventions, it is important not to label clients or their difficulties. Instead, try to explore clients' statements about their substance use, by drawing upon what they are saying at the time. This keeps any enquiry focused, manageable and client-centred. For example, a client mentions that he has been warned for smelling of drink again at work. He is more likely to elaborate on any concerns he may have about his alcohol use if the counsellor responds straightforwardly, by asking, for example, 'How do you feel about that?' or 'I wonder how that felt for you?' But if the counsellor at this point makes a direct enquiry about the client's drinking, however sensitively this is made, such as 'How do you feel about your drinking?', this is not close enough to what the client has said, and even if gently said may not be enough to facilitate further exploration, as it is too general a question for the client to be able to answer.

(ii)   Elaborating on this example further, if this client develops his story it is important to recognize and acknowledge overtly any felt concerns he may express around his drinking.

Equally, it is vital to empathize with any efforts to change. For example, if the client describes getting into the habit of drinking heavily each night to 'unwind', but then having to try to get to work in a reasonable state the next morning, the counsellor may respond to both the concern and the feelings with a simple empathic response: 'That feels like quite a struggle.' This is, of course, a straightforward counselling intervention, but it is useful in facilitating the particular point the client is making.

(iii) Equally, the counsellor should not empathize 'selectively', only responding in this way to certain parts of the client's overall story. It will soon become apparent to the client if a counsellor only affirms or empathizes with his or her expressions of concern or regret, especially if the counsellor tends to use affirmation and empathy as a technique, rather than out of genuine congruence. The counsellor also needs to be open to and empathic with those aspects of the client's drug and alcohol use that he or she enjoys, values, feels he or she cannot do without, and so on. A client's relationship to substance use cannot be divided neatly into good and bad parts: it is as complex as all human relationships.

Furthermore, the counsellor needs to be sensitive to clients' experiences of others towards them. To continue the example, while this client may understand being warned about smelling of alcohol at work as reasonable, he may also feel persecuted and scapegoated at a more personal level, because his drinking, which is of value to him, is under threat.

(iv)   In attending to the client's story, the counsellor needs to be mindful of any discrepancies that emerge. These include both feelings and facts. For example, early on in the session the client may describe feeling really good when smoking cannabis at night, and later mention that it leaves him lethargic in the mornings. Alternatively, a client may mention in passing that he enjoys a drink and never has any problems with it, yet later describe being arrested following a drunken brawl. Here the counsellor can, if it feels appropriate in the context of the session, bring the two conflicting feelings or facts together. This needs to be done gently to avoid giving the impression of 'catching the client out', which would clearly be unhelpful. Instead, the aim is to facilitate the client in recognizing differing, perhaps conflicting, aspects of his use of and relationship with alcohol and drugs, which can then be explored further.

(v) As already stated, it is unhelpful for the counsellor to label the client or to think in diagnostic terms. However, clients sometimes use these terms about themselves, often in a pejorative sense and 'out of the blue'. This can offer a natural place to intervene. In the example introduced above, the client may be talking about being warned for smelling of drink at work and then announce: 'Of course, they probably think I'm some sort of alcoholic.' If the counsellor is open and empathic at this point, this may help the client explore the more personal aspects of what he is saying about himself in making this statement.

(vi) The following interventions are particularly helpful, although they require an active and practical approach that may not rest easily with some counsellors. They are nonetheless interventions that the individual counsellor needs to consider using.

Sometimes clients do not appreciate or understand 'cause and effect', which links their substance use to other experiences. When it seems appropriate, explaining these links in a straightforward, pragmatic way can be liberating for the client. For example, a client, who drinks heavily every night, describes feeling anxious and sweaty every morning, attributing this to worries about the day ahead. The counsellor can explain the symptoms of withdrawal from alcohol, and simply offer this information to the client as an alternative explanation.

Some clients are open to the idea of keeping a record of their drink or drug use over a period of time to try to establish the 'facts' of their situation. Specific drink/drug diaries are readily available for this purpose. This should be presented only in the context of the client expressing the wish 'to know', not the counsellor wanting 'to show'.

Allied to this, formal measures such as blood tests, self-rating questionnaires and so on can help clients assess the nature and implications of their drink and drug use.

(vii) Finally, it needs to be appreciated that some clients may be helped in recognizing that their alcohol/drug use is problematic in an objective sense, while at the same time acknowledging that this does not constitute a problem that they wish to address at this time, or perhaps ever. As Rollnick and Bell (1991) have noted: 'Ultimately, the clients are the ones who decide what is best.'

Paul Jackson

* * *

3.3 I have heard of the need to take a very strict line when it comes to pointing out the way in which the client's drug use or drinking is really affecting him or her. Is this true?

It is not uncommon for drug-users to continue to use drugs, despite the fact that other people feel that their drug use repeatedly gives rise to serious consequences. Indeed, drug use may often continue despite the fact that the drug-user has acknowledged its repeated harmful consequences. Various models are advanced in order to account for the apparent anomaly between continued use and acknowledgement of harmful consequences. Perhaps most prominent in such explanations is the suggestion that drug-users have an exaggerated tendency to 'denial' when thinking about and/or discussing their drug use with others. The tendency to view denial as if it were a standard psychological attribute of addicts is very prominent within the 'disease models' of understanding addiction, and attempts to grapple with denial form a central part of treatment deriving from such approaches. It is suggested that it is only when the addict is able to both accept and surrender to the reality of the consequences of drug use that recovery becomes possible.

Although it is not uncommon for individuals to persist in using drugs despite adverse consequences, there are many other ways in which this apparent discrepancy may be articulated. In recent years, there has been enthusiasm for models derived from social learning theory, which tend to view apparent 'denial' as the product of the individual's interaction with others, rather than as a manifestation of an underlying (pathological) attribute. (See also Questions 5.1, 5.2, 5.3 and 5.4.)

Counsellors are generally concerned to avoid imposing labels and judgements upon their clients. They try instead to understand the uniquely personal significance of individual experience. To use the term 'denial' is to acknowledge that most people employ modes of 'denial', 'selective non-attention', 'avoidance', 'rationalization' and many other mechanisms in order to avoid distressing and awkward experiences. The

need to use such defences is partly contingent upon the imagined consequence of what would happen if we did not do so. Any individual who
anticipates difficult consequences is more likely to resort to various ways
of avoidance, whether in relating to self or to others. We know that it is
often as a result of the counsellor's ability to offer an accepting and non-
judgemental relationship that clients generally seem more able to engage
with their experiences more deeply and authentically.

In thinking about whether to adopt a 'strict line', as suggested by the
question, it is possible to adopt a more pragmatic and routine approach
when addressing areas of difficulty with clients who happen to use drugs. It
is important to ask who is responsible for asserting that a consequence of
drug use could be regarded as harmful, and for setting out what action
needs to occur as a result of such assertion. Few would disagree that it is
clients themselves who have the right and responsibility to decide how their
experiences ought to be perceived and categorized. However, there are
occasions where the counsellor feels that a client's progress will be restricted
until some currently difficult aspect of his or her experience can be faced.
In situations where a discrepancy exists between the current perceptions of
the client and the counsellor, an opportunity exists for exploration and
understanding – including the possibility that the counsellor may be wrong!

Within counselling approaches derived from the disease models of
understanding addiction, it is not uncommon for counsellors to adopt the
stance that they 'know best', and that disagreement with the counsellor's
point of view is the product of diseased or disordered thinking processes
on the part of the client, whose 'illness' will not permit acknowledgement
of the superior wisdom of the counsellor's opinions. It has to be noted
that many clients do regard this dynamic as helpful to them at certain
points in their attempts to resolve their drug problems.

Where the client appears not to acknowledge the harmful consequences of drug use, it is important for the counsellor to try to understand
why this is so. The reasons why clients may need or wish to avoid
acknowledging the consequences are fourfold, although these are
inevitably linked together in practice:

1. The client may possess *insufficient/deficient* information with which to
   appraise his or her experiences accurately. For example, a client may
   report great difficulty in sleeping, and describe how the use of a
   depressant drug such as alcohol or heroin helps in getting off to sleep,
   without understanding that the use of such drugs in itself may produce
   insomnia.

2. *Adaptational factors* may make it difficult for the client to see what is happening in new ways. The client who is experiencing regular withdrawal symptoms may not only fail to see that such symptoms are resulting from previous drug use, but may instead experience that the use of drugs actually relieves symptoms rather than being their cause. Similarly a client who socializes primarily with others who use his or her drug of choice regularly may experience a strong social pressure to focus on the positive, rather than the negative consequences of drug use.

3. The client may be subject to *intrapersonal dispositions* that make it difficult to acknowledge harm that may seem very evident to external observers. Some drug-users experience intense feelings of shame in acknowledging that continued drug use is causing problems for them. The potential for shame may be particularly threatening to those attempting to protect an already fragile sense of self-esteem. Some consequences of drug use are very frightening, and defences may be employed in order to avoid or minimize the fear that could result from a more complete acknowledgement of the effects of drug use.

4. The fourth reason for avoidance of this kind comprises *interpersonal factors* and is probably of particular relevance to counsellors. At the heart of many counselling approaches is the view that it is the quality of one's relationships with others that is of crucial importance in shaping personal experience, and in providing the means through which change may be possible, particularly within the therapeutic alliance. The more the counsellor is able to offer a committed and empathic relationship to the client, the more it will become possible for the client to engage in less restrictive forms of self-exploration, and enjoy the potential for change which can occur as a result. Clearly, the need for the provision of the 'core conditions', as described by Rogers (1957), becomes even more pronounced where the client may have to face potentially distressing aspects of the self.

Additionally, it is important that the counsellor should acknowledge that it is the client who is responsible for himself or herself, and that this includes the way that he or she uses drugs (see Question 7.2). In situations where the client behaves in ways that seem to show poor self-control or 'lack of conscience' there may be a particular temptation for the counsellor to adopt the role of 'external super-ego'. But as with other aspects of a client's life, it is not the counsellor's job to solve a client's problems, but rather to provide a caring and committed relational context, in which the client is better able to explore, understand and pursue alternative ways in which to conduct his or her life.

Although highly confrontational approaches to drug-using clients are not uncommon in some treatment facilities and environments, there is no empirical support to suggest that these have favourable outcomes (Hester and Miller 1989). The evidence is rather to the contrary. Highly confrontational approaches are likely to have unhelpful consequences for clients, including the potential for alienation, instead of engaging in a relationship where help is possible.

The counsellor who experiences undue difficulty in focusing upon difficult issues that arise during the work is unlikely to be able to offer the repertoire of skills adequate for the purpose of helping the client (Heron 1990). The capacity to maintain an honest and caring alliance within which difficult truths can be managed often achieves far more than the counsellor's attempts to impose his or her own view upon the client. The observations of attachment theory also indicate that experience of 'secure-base' conditions frees the individual to play and to explore more fully and creatively (Reading 2002).

Of course, like counsellors and everyone else, clients can make unwise decisions and avoid looking at what they need to see. Where confrontation seems necessary, a simple maxim that is of great value is 'Confront the issue, not the person!'

Bill Reading

* * *

3.4 I have a client who smokes cannabis before her sessions and tells me that she does this because it helps her to relax and talk about her feelings more easily. Is this something I should accept, particularly as I sometimes wonder how much she can really go into depth when she is like this?

This question contains two main elements: firstly, the question as to how this counsellor might manage the situation that is described; and secondly, the question of how deeply it is possible to work with the client under such circumstances. Let us first consider the question of depth and other potential effects upon the counselling process where the client attends intoxicated.

It does not seem that this particular client is so grossly intoxicated by cannabis that she is unable to attend or engage at all. However, any degree of intoxication is going to have some effects on the progress of the counselling relationship. This will be the case whatever drug is being used, though clearly, within counselling, particular drugs will have particular effects on what is possible (see Question 2.5).

Some might argue that to question a client's use of drugs may be counter to the principles of a 'client-centred' approach. However, it is not proposed that the counsellor should question or criticize a client's drug use in its entirety; rather that there may be a need to focus instead on the more particular circumstances, in which the client's drug use is having a direct impact on the process of counselling. Additionally, since a client-centred approach strives towards authentic engagement between client and counsellor, this is clearly likely to be limited if one or both of those present is under the influence of drugs.

The questioner states that the client feels that cannabis is helpful in both relaxing her and enabling her to talk about feelings. As counsellors, we are familiar with the observation that it is often the difficulties that inhibit expression of important areas of feeling and other experiences that are much more debilitating to the client than the content of what may be being avoided. We often observe the maxim from ego-psychology to the effect that we must work through 'resistance before content'. In other words, it is often the case that it is not the fact that the counsellor 'knows more about the client' which is the healing factor, but rather that the client is no longer subject to the fears and inhibitions that may formerly have been associated with unhelpful patterns of defence. Although drug use may reduce inhibition on some occasions, there is a risk that insufficient importance and attention is given to the defensive processes, which may be at work both within the client's approach to the counselling relationship and in relationships with important others in the client's life.

Of course, drug use affects not only what is expressed, but also the accompanying feelings. Cannabis provides us with a case in point. In addition to its relaxant properties, it also has hallucinogenic effects. Whilst these latter effects may be valued in some situations, they clearly represent a potential difficulty within counselling, in the sense that what the client describes will be subject to some degree of perceptual distortion as a result of intoxication. The talkativeness of a client on amphetamine, alcohol-assisted tears and the optimism of a cocaine user are easy examples of situations in which clients are likely to express themselves very differently when not under the influence of each of these particular drugs.

The fact that this counsellor needs to ask such a question suggests that drug use is already being experienced as a hindrance to communication with the client, and this may be particularly relevant in attempting to discuss the matter directly with the client. It may be, for example, that some drug-users demonstrate a fairly straightforward 'approach–avoidance conflict', in which attendance for counselling expresses a wish for intimacy and understanding, yet is conducted in such a way that these same possibilities are limited. Although the client's experiences are real enough when intoxicated, few would see them as having the same validity as experiences that occur unassisted and unmodified by the effects of drugs.

When we turn to the question of whether the counsellor should accept the situation, or find ways in which to manage it differently, it is worth considering some of the potential effects upon the counsellor's role-security when working with a client who is intoxicated. As has already been suggested, the client's intoxication is likely to limit the degree to which an encounter between the 'true selves' of client and counsellor becomes possible. The counsellor's capacity to use himself or herself creatively in the service of the client will be skewed by counter-transference feelings that may be evoked in this situation. The counsellor may feel de-skilled, hesitant, angry, or any combination of a number of emotions, in response to this situation. Of course, it may be that the evocation of such feelings in the counsellor provides a useful means of understanding what is happening with the client: for example, expressing the client's attempt to control levels of intimacy rather than take the risks that are implicit in a more direct form of engagement. Probably the single most prominent difficulty for the counsellor exists simply in the fact that he or she will not be able to discriminate between what is authentic and what is more properly seen as an artefact resulting from intoxication. The counsellor who is preoccupied with trying to solve this conundrum will be less fully available to listen to the client properly.

It would therefore clearly be helpful for the counsellor to accept the current position, but perhaps to find ways of working towards an improvement in the situation. It is neither necessary nor desirable to criticize or reject the client. Instead, the difficulties that intoxication present can be mutually acknowledged, reflected on and collaboratively addressed (see Question 3.5).

Many clients of course attend sessions under the influence of prescribed drugs such as antidepressants and tranquillizers. Many of the difficulties outlined above apply also to those under the influence of prescribed medication, although particular clients, counsellors and organizations will have differing views on these matters. In the best of circumstances, we aim to help clients engage more fully with themselves and to reduce their levels of 'psycho-phobia'. At least at a conceptual level, the client who is using mood-altering drugs to manage his or her experience may be subject to some degree of 'bi-modal relatedness', in the sense that prescribing and use of drugs may be an attempt to eliminate or modify certain experiences, whereas it is the counsellor's aim to facilitate a more direct contact with potential experience (Schachter 1993). Offering the client a relationship within which it becomes possible to disengage from drug use within the sessions may mark a crucial stage in the client's overall progress. As Guntrip once wrote:

> She took no medication at all on those mornings (of therapy), and would arrive feeling pretty ill, but always by the end of the session felt much better and found that a 'person' was better than a 'pill', a highly important discovery for her, as she had been under heavy medication for years.
>
> (Guntrip 1969: 338)

Bill Reading

* * *

3.5 Should I impose a clear rule on clients to insist that they attend drug- and alcohol-free?

This question has two aspects to it. Firstly, there is a situation such as that described in Question 3.4, in which the counsellor becomes aware that the client is attending under the influence of drugs. Secondly, there is the more general matter as to what posture the counsellor might adopt in addressing potential drug use by all clients.

Even where clients may have been assessed by a colleague elsewhere, the counsellor who is initiating contact with the client will be conducting some form of assessment, including the nature of the client's difficulties, whether these difficulties might be helped by counselling and what the particular focus and approach of counselling might be. Asking clients about their use of drugs and alcohol should form a routine part of the assessment process. It is extremely unlikely that any client uses no form of drugs whatsoever, even if this comprises only the occasional aspirin for a headache. At the other extreme, the magnitude of a client's drug use may be such as to represent a major factor in his or her life, including the very difficulties for which he or she is seeking help. As with other areas for potential exploration, it is important that the counsellor should feel sufficiently comfortable to ask the client about such matters. This can be done in a way that is neither intrusive nor persecutory (see Question 4.4).

Where it is clear at assessment that clients are using drugs very regularly, this provides the opportunity to explore the question of whether the client anticipates attending sessions under the influence of drugs. Although actual intoxication in sessions may cause some difficulty, empathic exploration of the client's relationship with drugs may grant the counsellor a privileged access to highly important and personal zones of a client's experience. We accept without difficulty that there are certain conditions that are highly conducive to the effectiveness of counselling, and others that are likely to hinder the process. A comfortable setting, privacy, confidentiality, freedom to pursue the relationship as much as it feels safe to do so, and the client's motivation to change matched by the counsellor's therapeutic commitment, are clearly amongst those factors likely to promote a satisfying and helpful relationship. The best possible conditions under which counselling might take place might include both counsellor and client being open to sensitive experiencing and exploration of all that unfolds between them. Intoxication on either or both parts will limit this potential.

I have yet to meet a client who has told me that he or she would prefer to see a counsellor who is intoxicated! When the roles are reversed in this way, the desirability of non-intoxication becomes self-evident. The respective roles of client and counsellor are very different, yet the relationship should be characterized by equality, which includes each of the parties carrying appropriate levels of responsibility. Viewed in this manner, it is difficult to see why counsellors are expected to observe a rule of non-intoxication whereas clients are not. Although allowing the client to attend sessions intoxicated might be regarded as somehow libertarian or respectful of the client's autonomy, it is easy to see that such a position is also patronizing, and negates the necessary degree of responsibility which clients must be able to bear in order to gain maximum benefit from the relationship. Although it is difficult to be precise in predicting the outcome of counselling, it is probably safe to say that there should be a sufficient conviction that the client is likely to benefit from the experience of counselling in order for the counsellor to feel congruent and committed to the process. The client who attends intoxicated may derive comfort and some value from sessions but it may be necessary to confront the fact that progress may be severely limited under such conditions. Both parties may feel that avoidance of this topic may be more comfortable and so permit the situation to continue. However, the counsellor should take particular care to distinguish between what promotes a productive collaboration, and what is more accurately viewed as a form of collusion, perpetuating a relationship which has little or no hope of achieving its aims.

One of the most prominent features of counsellor training and development is the emphasis on the establishment and maintenance of boundaries in order that the therapeutic alliance is likely to prosper. The counsellor is keen to provide a consistent relationship and setting in the knowledge that this will provide the 'secure base' within which counsellor and client can operate safely and productively.

Within my own practice, one of the most important learning processes has been that it is as a result of the counsellor's ability *to control the counselling context* that both client and counsellor are freed to conduct the necessary work. The counsellor must be able to control the appropriate aspects of the counselling situation for which he or she carries responsibility. Conversely, failure to control those aspects of the context appropriately almost inevitably leads to a situation in which the counsellor attempts instead to control the client! To take a simple example: the counsellor who cannot manage the boundary of time properly may be prone to concentrating on ways of ending the session with the current client before the imminent arrival of the next, rather than attending properly to what is actually happening 'in the moment'. We do not impose time limits on sessions in order to control the clients, but rather to liberate both them and ourselves from the need to be unnecessarily preoccupied with the question of time.

A client's decision to attend sessions drug-free is precisely that – a decision that the client is able to make. It is neither desirable nor necessary for this to represent an imposition on the part of the counsellor. Where the counsellor wishes the client to be drug-free during sessions, this constitutes an act of caring and a commitment to help the client achieve the goals towards which he or she is striving. There is wisdom in the following aphorism: 'Control the counselling context – not the client!'

Bill Reading

* * *

3.6 I have a client who regularly attends his sessions smelling of alcohol and who is sometimes quite unpredictable in mood. How should I raise this with him?

It is almost certain that this client has been consuming alcohol prior to the session. Recently consumed alcohol may smell quite strongly although at a relatively low dose, whereas the client who has been drinking very heavily the day before may smell only slightly of alcohol, despite still being quite heavily intoxicated. The question raises concerns not only about the client drinking but also the issue of the client's unpredictable mood, which may be closely related to the consumption of alcohol.

In asking this question, the counsellor is clearly experiencing some degree of anxiety as described in Questions 3.4 and 3.5. The counsellor probably senses that there may be difficulties in raising the question of the client's use of alcohol. It is possible that the counsellor may have personal reasons for finding this difficult, including previous situations with intoxicated individuals, difficulty with personal use of alcohol or a childhood experience of parental drinking. It is helpful for the counsellor to be able to identify and resolve potential taboos and anxieties that may be provoked in contemplating addressing this matter.

It is clearly crucial that the counsellor pays special attention to the question of his or her safety. The use of alcohol is particularly associated with increases in the potential for aggression: a client who when sober presents no risk may have the potential to become dangerous when drunk. It is invariably better to address the question of the client's drinking when the client is alcohol-free, or at least, relatively sober. A conversation which takes place when the client is drunk is much more likely to develop unhelpfully and involve some risk. Even where there seems no risk of actual violence, a client who is both intoxicated and emotionally aroused is much more likely to relate to the counsellor unproductively, without the ability to reflect usefully upon what is being said.

Although the counsellor may be able to see the ways in which the client's intoxication hinders the therapeutic alliance, it may be unhelpful to engage in premature interpretations as to the client's motives in using alcohol in this way. As an alternative, it is far more helpful for the counsellor to draw on his or her own experience, for example, advising the client of the difficulties which intoxication raises for the counsellor in attempting to help.

The client in this question may have real difficulty in getting to sessions alcohol-free, because he would otherwise experience marked withdrawal symptoms (see Questions 2.7 and 3.7). Once this topic has been broached, it is possible to discuss any difficulties that make it difficult for the client to attend without alcohol, as well as what might be done in order to help the client with this. For some, more specialist help may be required (see Questions 4.4 and 4.8). For many others, empathic exploration helps client and counsellor work together towards implementing change. There may be points at which cooperation between the counsellor and other helpers, such as the patient's general practitioner, may be desirable.

As with the response to Question 3.5, helping this client to attend his sessions alcohol-free should be seen as serving to help the client better, rather than as an attempt to control his behaviour.

The counsellor may need to consider some of the ethico-legal implications of working with clients who are known to be intoxicated. It may be helpful to refer to the Code of Ethics and Practice of any organization of which he or she is a member. Particular consideration needs to be given when the counsellor is aware that a client is driving a motor vehicle to and from sessions whilst intoxicated (see Question 7.1).

The counsellor needs to retain the right to terminate a relationship where it is considered unlikely to be productive and/or a risk to the safety and integrity of the client, counsellor or others. In extreme situations it may be better to communicate with the client on such matters by letter or telephone, in order to minimize any potential for difficulty within the face-to-face situation.

More optimistically, managing to find a way in which to discuss this client's drinking with him and to help him to bring about change may prove to be a significant milestone in the progression of the relationship towards achieving the patient's stated goals. My own experience is that clients are almost universally appreciative of the need to confront matters such as this in order to afford the counselling relationship the respect that it deserves.

Bill Reading

* * *

3.7 What if the client is so addicted or dependent that getting to sessions without drugs is impossible?

It can happen that a client may state that it is 'impossible' to attend sessions without being under the influence of drugs. Before discussing situations where such a statement must be taken at face value, it is worth considering other factors that may come into play when a client says this.

Some clients use drugs so regularly that they have little or no experience in recent times of doing anything without being under their influence. Similarly others may have undergone cognitive adaptation (see Question 2.1) as a result of which they come to believe that taking drugs has become necessary in certain situations, or in order to cope with life in general. Even where the client reports that drug use has a 'compulsive' quality, it is important that the counsellor should not overlook the part the client's choice plays in taking drugs and should therefore explore the reasons that support such a choice. For many clients, it can be very liberating to acknowledge the difference between a feeling that no choice is possible and the (gradual) recognition that some degree of choice remains open to them. A belief that it is 'not possible' to attend sessions drug-free is clearly likely to influence a client's behaviour in that direction. It requires skill for the counsellor both to acknowledge the client's feelings of passivity (regarding drug use), whilst simultaneously relating to the client as autonomous and with the capacity for decisions. Rather than making the mistake of moving into an 'either/or' discussion (i.e. 'compelled' or 'choosing') the counsellor needs to be able to empathize with the different levels of experience that almost certainly exist, given the complex nature of the relationship between the drug and the drug-user (e.g. knowing one has a choice, yet feeling *compelled* to act in a particular way).

Many years ago Wurmser (1978) suggested that some drug-users may attempt to engage in what he termed 'the Invalidating Fantasy' when organizing their relationships with helpers. Essentially, this is when certain interactions with others are geared towards neutralizing the recognition that drug use is problematic and that some change is required. The client who insists that it is not possible to function without drugs may be seeking the counsellor's compliance in consolidating such an Invalidating Fantasy, whether intentionally or by default.

The counsellor's failure to question the client's basis for making such an assertion may be experienced as lending further credence to the view that drug use has become routine, and that there is a decreasing basis for assuming that change is possible – a further cognitive adaptation to drug use: for example, 'My counsellor agrees that it would be unreasonable to expect me to attend sessions without taking drugs.'

Situations in which drug-free attendance is impossible or difficult are almost certainly explicable either in terms of the client's gross intoxication (in which case counselling is extremely unlikely to be a credible option) or where the client is likely to experience severe withdrawal symptoms unless continuing to use the drug (see Question 2.7). Although often unpleasant, withdrawal from drugs is not dangerous in the majority of cases, and is always transient. For many clients the support and encouragement of those around them may be sufficient, and superior to withdrawal assisted by medication or hospitalization.

Where it is clear that withdrawal would be dangerous and/or extremely difficult to achieve, the counsellor can help by supporting the client in obtaining appropriate help, or even taking a more active role in helping the client make contact with other services. The counsellor who has an adequate understanding of commonly used drugs and their respective withdrawal symptoms is better equipped to judge these situations.

Those clients who require medical/hospital intervention in order to withdraw from drugs and those undergoing withdrawal currently/recently will benefit more from the counsellor's supportive interventions, with more 'expressive' interventions being less helpful at this stage (Luborsky 1984). More specifically, withdrawal from drugs may represent a period of particular fragility for the client. Techniques and approaches that might further stress the client during this phase ought to be used only with extreme caution. Moreover, many apparent symptoms and other phenomena that might be of interest to the counsellor may change very substantially and spontaneously as a client successfully withdraws from drugs. Marked feelings of depression, paranoia, emotional lability or agitation may require little more than the counsellor's ability to contain them as they start to reduce during the withdrawal phase. A competent discrimination between features that have a bona fide claim upon the counsellor's attention, and those that have been artefacts secondary to symptoms of intoxication or withdrawal, is often only possible some weeks after the client has successfully managed to withdraw.

In some situations the client may continue to take mood-altering drugs throughout counselling, particularly where he or she is being advised to continue a prescription whilst continuing in counselling. In such situations (e.g. the prescribing of methadone to opiate users), the counsellor may need to modify both the approach that is adopted and the goals it is hoped will be achieved as a result of counselling. An obvious example might be a situation in which it is clear that the client needs to be able to access certain emotions in order to work through a particular difficulty, yet where the capacity to experience feeling is limited by the use of drugs such as methadone.

Bill Reading

* * *

3.8 I am seeing a female client who tells me that her husband's drinking is causing her immense anxiety. Is help available for people in her position in addition to the help she can get from counselling?

There is help available to people in this and similar situations beyond that provided by general counselling. One of the best known and important of these is Al Anon, which is an equivalent organization to Alcoholics Anonymous, but which is for the partners and relatives of drinkers. Al Anon groups first emerged in America during the 1950s, being the brainchild of Lois W, wife of Bill W, who was one of the founders of AA. Aware of the distress and suffering caused to spouses who were living with alcoholics, she wanted to reach out to other wives of alcoholics. Since that time, Al Anon, like AA, has become a worldwide organization, but is no longer confined to spouses or indeed to women. Al Anon reaches out to *anyone* who believes that they have been affected by the drinking or alcoholism of someone to whom they are close, be it a partner, a spouse, a sibling, a parent or a friend. There is a network of such groups in Britain, and the client in the question could be encouraged to find out about her local meetings by telephoning Al Anon. For those affected by someone else's *drug* use, the appropriate organization to contact is Families Anonymous, which runs along similar principles (see Dorn et al. 1987).

The other practical suggestion is for the counsellor to consider contacting local addiction services, such as a local alcohol service or community drug unit. Although such services are set up to provide interventions for those who are using alcohol or other substances, some units also provide specialist opportunities for those affected by addiction, in the form of individual sessions and/or groups. Likewise, some residential addiction programmes provide opportunities for family members to be directly involved in the care of someone struggling with addiction and recovery. Joint sessions involving the user, and separate or unilateral interventions, excluding the user, can help.

Clients with such concerns are usually overwhelmed by worry. Presenting for help may be one of a number of efforts over a period of time to try to change the behaviour of their loved one. This is the usual starting point, the relative or spouse trying to influence or to control the drinker or desperately trying to contain a situation of increasing crisis. The client may hope that the counsellor can provide a magical solution or advice through which the recalcitrant drinker might finally accept treatment or the need for change. It is rather as though they are searching for the missing piece to a jigsaw. It is helpful for the counsellor to ask the client for a full history of the drink-related problems that have been experienced, and to ask about incidents and crises. Relatives may experience shame, or think that they have exaggerated the problems, so accurate reflection around the difficulties they have experienced is essential. Has violence been involved, and if so of what kind? Are there children, and if so how have their needs been protected? What are their financial worries? Has the relative tried to make appointments or arrange treatment for the drinker? Have they tried to cover up the practical and emotional mess caused by the drinking? Have they kept the problems quiet or have they managed to communicate their concerns to others? What is *their* use of alcohol?

The next step is to reflect empathically on the consequences entailed in trying to manage such worries. Invariably, there will have been a gradual cost in terms of the client's own needs or in those of the family as a whole. Social contacts, leisure activity, mental and physical health may all have been affected, and as the addiction progresses some relatives may find themselves submerging or sacrificing their needs almost entirely in an attempt to deal with or help the user. Helping the individual to acknowledge this may be an important part of validating their experience. Many relatives will have been bullied or blamed by the drinker, and so may have come to doubt their own judgement. At the same time, it is important to explore *how* the individual has become caught up and may have become co-opted into the world and activities of the substance abuser. Some professionals talk about the concept of 'co-dependency' (Cermak 1989), referring to the way in which a relative becomes dependent on dysfunctional relationship patterns or the need to try to control other people.

There are two main aims in offering help to relatives: to help the person overcome denial and to be able to face the painful reality of addiction in a loved one; and to help that person to reclaim his or her own needs and to be reminded of his or her choices in given relationships or situations. The relationship and time spent with the counsellor can be viewed as a space away from the immediate pressures of domestic life, through which the individual is encouraged to gain a sense of objectivity and perspective. Similarly, Al Anon talk about the importance of achieving some measure of detachment from the situation as the only means of protecting the mental health of the involved relative. This is sometimes labelled 'tough love'. But there are usually no simple solutions at hand.

Martin Weegmann

* * *

3.9 One of my clients suffered severe sexual abuse as a child and feels that she will not be able to stop drinking until she has come to terms with her past. Is this true?

Recent studies in the United Kingdom suggest the prevalence of childhood sexual abuse to be 12 per cent for females and 8 per cent for males. It is thought that the incidence rate for males is significantly under-reported (Berry 2000). The association between child sexual abuse and later substance abuse is empirically supported (Finkelhor and Browne 1986). Further, in major research reviews Finkelhor and Browne (1986) conclude that around 40 per cent of sexually abused children suffer consequences serious enough for them to seek formal help of some description in adulthood.

Counsellor factors

Working with clients who have been sexually abused as children promotes extremely powerful responses in the counsellor, which are well documented. Similarly, working with clients who present with substance misuse problems often promotes strong reactions in counsellors. However, the client who has been both abused as a child and has a substance misuse problem as an adult can precipitate very specific, conflicting, and ambivalent feelings in the counsellor. At the risk of over-

simplification, the conflict is around experiencing the wish to both perse-
cute and rescue the very person we are meant to be helping. Initially,
victims of sexual abuse engender powerful nurturing, loving and protective feelings, whereas those who misuse substances are likely to prompt
more hostile and judgmental responses. Counsellors cannot afford to split
off the different experiences in themselves that arise in response to the
whole person of the client.

Substance misuse in context

Despite being accepted, the association between childhood sexual abuse
and later substance misuse has not been explored and remains largely at
the level of noting the connection. The general conclusion is that
substances are used in an attempt to cope with the traumatic consequences of the abuse. Whilst not in disagreement with this as a baseline of
understanding, the use of substances is invariably more complex and it
usually emerges over time that the client is doing much more than trying
to block off painful experiences. For example, Hall and Lloyd (1989)
make the following three observations:

1. Victims of sexual abuse never learn appropriate ways of dealing with
   their anger and often turn it inwards, expressing this through alcohol
   and drug misuse, self-mutilation and suicide attempts.
2. The consequence of nightmares, ranging from a fear of going to sleep
   to suicide attempts may involve increased self-mutilation, running
   away and drug and alcohol misuse.
3. In the days following the disclosure of the abuse, or some aspect of it,
   the client may attempt suicide, abuse alcohol or drugs heavily, or muti-
   late themselves in some way.

Substance misuse, therefore, can not only be understood as a way of
defending against feelings, but also one of the many consequences of 'failing' to defend against feelings.

To ask or not to ask

Given the known prevalence of childhood sexual abuse in clients who
develop substance misuse problems, this issue cannot be ignored.
However, it is clearly not helpful to ask in a routine, unempathic or
ambiguous way whether abuse has occurred. Instead, any enquiry must
be in context, emerging out of what the client has been saying. If the

counsellor feels strongly that abuse has happened, if the therapeutic relationship seems secure and if any enquiry can be related to the here-and-now, only then is it appropriate to ask about the possibility of earlier abuse. Jackson (1996) suggests that intervening in this manner conveys at least three important statements:

1. The client 'hears' that talking about their sexual abuse is an appropriate part of this therapeutic relationship.
2. The counsellor has demonstrated the belief in their ability to 'be' with the client.
3. A safety and security in the therapeutic setting is implied.

What to work with and when

The counsellor frequently has to struggle with what in the client's presentation they respond to first, and on what basis they make this decision. In this instance, the substance misuse is likely to be part of the presenting difficulties, and the sexual abuse both an immediate and underlying causative factor. It is difficult for the counsellor to strike the balance between responding either in a collusive or persecutory manner. For example, the counsellor may collude with unaddressed substance misuse, considering it is the only way the client can cope with their pain. Alternatively, they may insist on very rigid, patently unrealistic treatments that focus entirely on the client's alcohol/drug misuse, leaving the abuse unaddressed. Logic suggests that clients should try to establish a period of stability with regard to their substance use in order to work usefully with their experience of abuse. However, in reality it is rarely this ordered, and the client and counsellor often take a more pragmatic view, and work on both concurrently within agreed defined parameters. These parameters relate to 'how' the client attends for counselling (see Questions 3.4 and 3.5), in what way the substance misuse is addressed, and how working on the sexual abuse is balanced with this. The substance misuse and sexual abuse are not responded to as discrete entities that coexist, but rather as experiences that reside within the same person and are expressed interactively. This conceptual 'bringing together' can be very enabling for clients as they start to understand the way their substance misuse can perpetuate and often repeat many facets of their earlier abuse.

    This is obviously a difficult balance to maintain and it has to be acknowledged that this is rarely a smooth process. There is sometimes an almost imperceptible difference between a client's substance use, in which they are engaged in something self-destructive, and something that is self-preserving. So if a client misses several sessions because of their drug use or drinks heavily immediately after each meeting, it is not enough to interpret this solely as evidence that their substance misuse is out of control, although sometimes this is the case. Instead, as with any difficulty encountered in counselling, its meaning needs to be discussed and understood in context. Allied to this, the intensity of feelings engendered often leads to the obvious being lost and faulty attributions being made. There is no evidence to suggest that victims of childhood sexual abuse per se are more or less able to make healthy changes to their substance misuse than those who have not been abused. Furthermore, relapse is a regular occurrence in treatment, so that relapse in itself should not be viewed as being of greater or lesser significance in those clients that have been abused in childhood. As always, it is the individual person who must be responded to.

Remembering and communicating

There is sometimes a reluctance to attribute any great significance to what clients do, think and feel when under the influence of substances. However, to assume this behaviour is an arbitrary consequence of being intoxicated is therapeutically limiting for both client and counsellor, particularly when this behaviour seems to replicate or perpetuate abusive experiences. Disowning experiences in this way is a further form of dissociation and disengages clients from deeply personal aspects of themselves. When the counsellor demonstrates the wish to know and accept these aspects of the client, this can be an immensely important step towards the client's own integration. Furthermore, the client's intoxicated behaviour often appears to be part of a long-standing, repeated cycle, which might be understood in dynamic terms as the attempt to communicate what they also cannot bear to tell. Perhaps the more the client is able to be in touch with these aspects of themselves, the less need there is to enact them when intoxicated.

We also know that many clients enter counselling without any conscious memory of being abused and that this may emerge in the course of therapy. This has particular relevance as substances are used regularly for their dissociative properties, and a period of abstinence or reduced consumption may precipitate recall, or partial recall. This is often followed by a return to heavy substance use in an attempt to dissociate again. However, relapse need not follow relapse indefinitely. If the client feels safely held therapeutically, and the counsellor does not search, intrude or work specifically on the suspected abuse, then the client may be more able to gain stability in their substance use and tolerate increased recall of their abuse. But it is vital that the counsellor does not act intrusively during this process. As Dale (1999) notes, there is a need to provide clients with the opportunity to talk about abuse if they so wish, while avoiding being over inquisitive or invasive.

Paul Jackson

* * *

3.10 I have assessed a client who tells me that she attends meetings of Narcotics Anonymous and that she has a sponsor there. Is this likely to conflict with the work we might attempt within counselling?

The question of the relationship between self-help or fellowship organizations such as Narcotics Anonymous and professional counselling is an interesting one. In decades gone by, there was often a mutual tension between the cultures of fellowship organizations and the professional world of therapy, counselling and psychiatry. Some in fellowship organizations adopted anti-professional views, believing that only fellow addicts and the strength provided by the mutual support of addicts could be effective. For others, there was a suspicion that the professional world had its own prejudice against addicts and that professional interventions might reinforce an addict's denial or defiance, or both. On the professional side, however, it could argued that there was considerable ignorance about the nature of addiction and about the growing significance of AA and other similar organizations at that time. Some professionals were no doubt wary of the religious or spiritual language used, or saw such organizations as cults; others might have been critical of people 'replacing' addiction to drugs, through supposed dependence on attending self-help groups (Tiebout 1944; Kinney and Montgomery 1979).

Although prejudice or lack of awareness still exists in this area, there is now a culture of far more cooperation and respect. Fellowship organizations make no bones about their limitations and about the importance of members pursuing professional help where needed. Their attitude could be characterized as non-interference. At the same time they pride themselves on being a non-professional organization with the simple aim of reaching out to fellow addicts who are still suffering. The approach to recruitment is one of 'attraction rather than promotion'.

Likewise, most counsellors and therapists nowadays are likely to take a supportive and pragmatic attitude towards fellowship organizations and encourage such affiliations where needed.

Sponsoring within NA or AA involves a newcomer or an attendee being assigned another person of the same gender who has travelled further along the path of recovery. It is a form of peer support, informal contact and guidance. The individual may simply phone or meet their sponsor as difficulties arise, or the sponsor may spend time helping the individual through the different 'steps' of recovery. There are Twelve Steps in fellowship organizations, through which the individual committed to sobriety might progress. The starting point, Step One, is the basic acknowledgement that the person's life had become unmanageable as a result of the use of alcohol or substances.

A pragmatic response to the situation described in the question is firstly to learn more about what led this client towards affiliation with Narcotics Anonymous, and to acknowledge the aspects which he or she finds helpful in such an approach; and secondly to ask more about the client's relationship to the sponsor, picking up any sources of difficulty, as well as acknowledging what he or she find helpful. The therapeutic role of non-professional peers should not be underestimated. Finally, explore whether the client or the sponsor might sense any potential conflict between the different approaches and ask whether it has been discussed with the sponsor and/or fellowship. It is important to understand what is meaningful to the client, but also to be aware of the risk of splitting, so it might be important to explore why the person seeks professional help at this particular juncture.

Martin Weegmann

* * *

3.11 How can I tell if someone I believe is an addict is being honest with me? I've heard that such clients are inclined to lie about their habits.

It is important that we meet all our clients with optimal openness and acceptance: the starting point of all clinical work is to gain an understanding of what the client is presenting with and why. Prejudices – acknowledged or unacknowledged – exist in all fields of mental health and people with addictions can be pre-judged in particular ways. Among the risks are that addicts are seen as homogeneous, or are seen as universally dishonest, manipulative and unmotivated. The word 'lying' has similar pejorative connotations. It is sometimes easier to discern such attitudes in professional groups other than our own, e.g. GPs or generic psychiatrists, but we need to remember that we may also share such attitudes, even unconsciously. This could reflect an absence of direct experience with addicted individuals – prejudice and ignorance are bedfellows – and may reflect a lack of skill or ability in assessing an addiction objectively.

On the other hand, it is important not to be gullible and, as with any client, to maintain a realistic and reflective stance. We should remember that with clients where dishonesty is an issue, they are also showing us their difficulty in being honest with, or in living with, themselves. This might constitute a focus for the initial exploration.

As for this question, it is important to assess, as with any other client, in what context the referral comes, and from this to form an initial sense of what might have brought the client to therapy (Weegmann 2001). Secondly, it is one thing to suspect one is dealing with an 'addict', but this is a shorthand label, and in fact we are dealing with an individual who may be struggling with an addiction. More significantly, what is the client's view of his or her predicament and use of substances or alcohol? It is obviously important to have some knowledge and training (even of a basic kind) about the nature of addiction and to be able to make a provisional assessment of this. This needs to be done in a tactful gently enquiring way, rather than a confrontational or oppositional manner.

We therefore need to build up a picture of what clients bring – their attitude towards their situation – together with what they might be asking us to respond to. Is there, for instance, an immediate crisis or is there external pressure? Whose idea was the appointment? Motivational issues are crucial to assess where addiction is concerned (Rollnick and Miller 1995). However, motivation cannot be thought of a single trait, which is either present or absent: it is best thought of as a complex continuum, with different degrees of readiness and ability to change. There is now a strong tradition in the field of addiction concerning the need to carefully understand the motivational state(s) of the addicted person and to assist in preparing people to be able to change. Simply enabling an individual to contact a specialist addiction service might be one example of a good outcome as a result of motivational facilitation.

An addiction constitutes, by definition, a compulsive activity over which conscious control becomes weakened. If we use the metaphor of a gang, we could suggest that any addiction is a powerful state and is defended at all cost: it resists pressure from other people to change, and it finds methods to reduce perceived dissonance or conflicts about the consequences of continuing. In a way, there is a kind of mental 'closing of ranks' that serves to protect the addiction, until perhaps things begin to fall apart or a continuation of resistance is less viable for personal, social or physical reasons. Although honesty may well be one of the victims in this effort to maintain an addiction, it is more helpful to think in terms of the individual's attempts to disavow the more painful aspects of his or her activities. As a result the individual may well present in a defensive manner, and hide behind illusions about himself or herself, which is why considerable sensitivity is required in order to get closer to the person. To continue the gang metaphor, the therapist is trying to form an alliance with the part of the individual that might want change, in order to diffuse the power or omnipotence of the rest of the gang. The counsellor unself-consciously models the value of an honest relationship. He or she might even be thought of as a kind of honest broker between the individual, the addiction and the prospect of change.

Martin Weegmann

CHAPTER 4

Generic models and specialist training in addictions counselling

4.1 I am familiar with different theoretical models that are used in generic counselling. Can these models be used when working with addicted clients?

Some generic counsellors tend to use a fairly pure theoretical approach whilst others adopt a much more eclectic position, drawing on aspects of differing theories that seem to have value when attempting to help a client at a particular point in time. Many writers and theorists have adapted ideas from some of the more prominent schools of psychology and counselling for use when working with clients who use drugs (Edwards and Dare 1996; McMurran 1994). Such modifications of theory pick up the underlying assumptions that are typical of the model in question. For example, a psychodynamic model is likely to be concerned with the role of unconscious factors as determinants of addiction, and the resolution of some aspects of the problem through transference analysis. A counsellor using tenets of systemic theory may tend to consider substance use in terms of its role in maintaining a state of homeostasis within the family, with therapy aimed at helping the system realign in ways that do not require ongoing substance misuse.

It is often possible to achieve an economy of hypothesis in the sense that much can be explained quite simply in terms of the client's current relationship with the drug of choice. For example, continuing substance use in order to avoid otherwise difficult withdrawal symptoms may offer a far more potent explanatory model than either powerful unconscious process or cybernetic family systems.

In more recent years, there has been a move away from considering those who use substances problematically as representing a distinct client group towards drawing on more established and generic models of understanding. In one sense, it is a move away from the notion of 'addicts' to that of 'people who use substances' – i.e. that drug-users remain people first and foremost. It has been clear for some decades that therapists of various persuasions produce better outcomes when they can be shown to be deploying the core conditions (Hubble et al. 1999). There is much to suggest that clients who misuse substances benefit similarly if able to enjoy the provision of these 'relationship variables' regardless of any particular theoretical leanings that the counsellor may have (Najavits and Weiss 1994). While one cannot overlook the potential for differing degrees of usefulness across theories, it is important to note that theory exists not only as something with which to assist the client but also as a means by which counsellors and therapists are able to maintain feelings of security and competence.

Consideration is given in the answer to Question 4.7 to a model within which it is possible to consider whether a particular approach might be more suitable for a particular client. Further discussion of the relative effectiveness of differing approaches can be found in the answer to Question 4.2.

Attempts to research both generic and substance misuse-specific counselling outcomes have tended repeatedly to suggest that it is the relationship variables rather than the theoretical approach which have a more potent effect upon engagement, retention and eventual outcome for counselling and therapy. Those working with clients who use drugs share with generic colleagues the acknowledgement that it is the quality of 'being with' the client rather than the process of 'doing to' the client which should be the first concern.

Bill Reading

* * *

4.2 Is there any evidence to suggest that some approaches have more effective outcomes than others in addictions counselling?

This question involves the complex topic of 'evidence-based practice'. Increasingly, it is a term with which counsellors and all those working in the alcohol and drugs field are required to be familiar. The concept emerged first in general medicine in the United Kingdom and USA, spread across to mental health, and is now beginning to gain ground in the psychological therapies (Department of Health 2001; Roth and Fonagy 1996). It has also extended from the health service into private and voluntary organizations as well as into the criminal justice system – and so, inevitably, the addictions field needs to look seriously at its own position vis-à-vis approaches that might vary in their effectiveness.

Those who support this trend point out that it is both necessary and ethically responsible to move away from the so-called 'postcode lottery' in the provision of services. No matter where they live, people should be able to rely on being offered care or treatment that achieves an acceptable standard. Those who deliver it are accountable to the tax-payer and to their clients or patients: their practice should be open to external scrutiny and based on methods chosen for their effectiveness, not on personal ideology, habit or hunches that cannot be articulated or justified. Clinical judgements need to be based on understanding theory and research in one's field of practice. Those who make these very persuasive points also refer to studies such as that of Norcross and Prochaska (1983), which indicate that conscious application of research about what is known to be effective is one of the least significant factors for clinicians in selecting their counselling style (see also Harris 2001).

Does it therefore follow that the argument in favour of only paying attention to evidence-based practice in addictions counselling is irrefutable? The proposal put forward here is that we need to think about how the terminology used in questions about what works may have to be re-interpreted to fit with who and what we are investigating. There is much that is ambiguous in this field and we are still feeling the way. There are in fact many aspects of counselling and therapy that are simply not compatible with the positivist medical model, which set the scene originally for evidence-based effectiveness research. There are also crucial ethical dimensions: we need to care for individuals experiencing addiction problems, whether or not successful methods of 'curing' or 'controlling' them have been identified. Other reasons for re-thinking existing ways of tackling the issue are discussed below, and the reader is directed to some of the literature that describes the current state of play regarding research evidence.

Defining 'approaches'

Attempting to discover which specific factor of a service has potency leads to questions of how words are defined. In the descriptive and research literature in the addictions field of the last 30 years, there are references to approaches or interventions drawn from a wide range of categories. They include social, psychiatric and spiritual approaches; these either co-exist with, or are in contrast to the 'talking therapies'. There have been attempts to evaluate self-help movements (e.g. Alcoholics Anonymous), pharmacotherapy (e.g. methadone maintenance programmes), treatment defined by its milieu (e.g. residential therapeutic communities), treatment defined by its length (e.g. so-called brief interventions) as well as non-directive counselling, behavioural and cognitive approaches, and psycho-dynamic therapy. There are interventions that are wholly or mainly designed to be used with people with addiction problems, such as 'brief interventions', 'bibliotherapy', social behaviour and network therapy, motivational interviewing, motivation enhancement therapy and Twelve-Step facilitation. 'Approaches' is an all-encompassing word that has been used to refer to theoretical model, length of intervention and setting – each of which needs to be investigated separately whilst the other variables are held constant. This does not often occur in addictions research.

Defining 'addictions counselling'

What do practitioners, researchers and policy-makers understand by the activity labelled 'addictions counselling'? One source of confusion is that the counselling world and the addictions field tend to use different languages to define their activities, making comparisons and generalizations difficult. The addictions field is essentially multi-disciplinary, and subject to political and public pressures, with powerful influences (including legislation and the selective provision of resources) being exerted at particular times. For example, in the 1980s in the United Kingdom there was a strong public health agenda for drug services: Aids and HIV were spreading and money was made available in an attempt to curtail infection amongst injecting drug-users through, for example, 'harm minimization' – counselling skills and an emphasis on education. By the beginning of the new century, the political agenda in England and Wales shifted the focus on to reducing crime associated with illicit drug use, and the terminology and framework of the criminal justice system permeated the provision of help for drug users. Coercion has become an implicit or explicit aspect of many interventions – a factor highly likely to undermine the establishing of a genuinely collaborative therapeutic relationship. The term 'counselling' is thus often inaccurate to describe activities in these settings.

The counselling world, although it is theoretically diverse and overlaps in sometimes confusing ways with psychotherapy, has a reasonably clear sense of what its core activity is. It emphasizes that the use of counselling skills is different from counselling. It is based on therapeutic alliance that is freely entered into. It is far less affected by political pressures and by treatment fashions than the addictions world. Nonetheless, in the United Kingdom, the term 'counselling' is consistently used to refer to an activity that is assumed to be an integral part of any programme providing help for alcohol- or other drug-users. It was reported as being a 'key treatment' in 94 per cent of the community drug agencies surveyed as part of the NTORS study in 1996. This survey, however, also found that the agencies did not differentiate between formal counselling and 'support' – a fundamental consideration if effectiveness of approaches is to be explored or compared. The NTORS survey found that only three out of 18 agencies would satisfy the British Association for Counselling and Psychotherapy's definition of counselling. The areas in which most of them failed to meet the criteria were levels of qualification and training of counsellors, and their inability to articulate the nature of the approach they used. This latter point – which does not imply that they were in any way incompetent – creates real difficulty in comparative research studies.

Some of the research literature in the United Kingdom and North America equates the term 'counselling' with a theoretical stance – see, for example, Roth and Fonagy (1996), who attempt to summarize the effectiveness of counsellors' interventions in primary care settings (not specifically in relation to addictions). They state that the 'blurring of professional background and psychological technique makes it difficult to be clear about the relationship between treatment and outcome in these studies' (1996: 341). This pragmatic approach to the term 'counselling' in outcome research into the psychological therapies is also reflected in much of the addictions treatment effectiveness research prior to 1997. A trawl through the limited number of North American research articles where effectiveness of counselling is discussed reveals phrases such as 'traditional counselling', 'standard counselling' and 'drug counselling versus professional psychotherapy'. One can only guess at what the researchers – and the practitioners – mean by these activities.

One of the complex elements in disentangling what is delivered when, by whom, in what settings, is the possibility that in the United Kingdom today this may depend on whether practitioners in the addictions field are recruited from counselling/psychotherapy training courses, or whether they have no formalized training, or whether they have in-service training on addiction-specific interventions such as motivational interviewing. If they have had training in a particular theoretical model, they are more likely to describe the work they do in those terms. Thus, what is done by addiction counsellors may in fact include systemic interventions with couples and families, solution-focused therapy, person-centred counselling, cognitive-behavioural interventions and behavioural interventions. Some of the outcome research in the alcohol field has compared some of these different models ('approaches'), but this has not been the norm for studies of treatment of other drug problems. At the same time, as indicated above, it may be that most of the counselling that takes place is eclectic in nature – perhaps also varying according to a client's position in the 'cycle of change' (see Question 5.3), or to other criteria of need identified by the practitioner.

Problems in 'effective outcomes' research

As has been pointed out in the psychotherapy literature, the metaphor in which 'talking therapies' are equated with providing medication to treat physical illnesses has many limitations when undertaking research into effectiveness – but it nonetheless remains the dominant model. The so-called 'gold standard' for proving whether one pharmacological treatment is superior to another in treating an illness is the randomized controlled trial. This approach is ubiquitous too in evaluating outcomes in psychotherapy and the addictions, but the difficulties of ensuring methodological purity, and the question marks surrounding applicability to everyday practice, are enumerated in many reviews (Heather 1996). Counselling and psychotherapy writers are increasingly arguing that these flaws can only be addressed by finding alternatives to randomized controlled trials, including greater use of qualitative rather than quantitative research (Hubble et al. 1999). However, drug and alcohol research is extremely low on the list of funding priorities for health and social care services in this country, and it is unrealistic to think that any large-scale, robust outcome study that does not fit within the conventional medical model would be adequately funded.

The fallacy that psychotherapy and counselling interventions can be evaluated as if they were pharmacological interventions is most obvious (and arguably most clearly discredited) in the preoccupation with comparing effectiveness of one theoretical model of therapy with another. The talking therapies consist of human interaction – a dynamic interplay of mutual influence. It was in the 1970s that the phrase 'Everyone has won, and all shall have prizes' was adopted (from *Alice in Wonderland*) to sum up the empirical evidence that no psychotherapeutic model has been shown to be superior in outcome to any other. However, resources continue to be put into re-exploring this type of research.

As well as there being some important question marks about *what* is being asked, there is also the matter of *how* the research is carried out and how results are *interpreted* and applied. Heather (1996) describes replicability and standardization as two major methodological problems to be resolved in attempting to evaluate effectiveness. Researchers seldom reach consensus on how crucial variables should be defined, measured and reported. There is also the difficulty of ensuring adequate control groups, sample sizes being too small; and the need for using a wide spectrum of matching variables in order to establish what works best for whom. Then there is the complex question of the extent to which even well-conducted research results can be regarded as relevant to most treatment settings in the United Kingdom today. Many of the studies that are quoted are 'efficacy' studies (involving manualized therapy, random assignment to treatment and control groups, a fixed number of sessions, well-operationalized target outcomes, participants meeting criteria for a single diagnosed disorder) – by definition, seeking maximum internal validity. But as Seligman points out, this is 'the wrong method for empirically validating psychotherapy as it is actually done, because it omits too many crucial elements of what is actually done in the field' (1995: 966). What actually is carried out in the name of treatment – and arguably this is particularly true in relation to addictions counselling – is untested. Seligman argues that the way to overcome the idea that effectiveness of treatment as delivered in 'the real world' cannot ever be empirically validated is to use a different method. He describes the advantages of well-conducted effectiveness studies, such as a major survey conducted by Consumer Reports (1995). The value of this approach, too, is that the experience of the client himself or herself is accessed directly.

Project MATCH

Project MATCH was undertaken during the 1990s in the USA in order to test ideas about matching clients seeking help for alcohol problems with the most suitable treatment approach. In this case 'approach' referred to a limited number of sessions of either cognitive-behaviour therapy, motivational enhancement therapy, or Twelve-Step facilitation, delivered by a trained practitioner in either an in-patient or an out-patient specialist treatment setting (Project MATCH 1997). It was the biggest and most expensive psychotherapy outcome evaluation ever conducted, and the methodology was extremely rigorous. Many commentators regard the findings as disappointing, but in terms of the question posed in this section, it served to clarify that the effectiveness of alcohol counselling was unlikely to be improved by matching clients to particular theoretical approaches. All the research participants in fact did well and there are a variety of views about why this was the case. A persuasive argument, in the light of findings in the psychotherapy outcome literature, is that the three treatments were in fact similar in a crucial dimension: a high level of working alliance was achieved in all three groups. This result echoes much of the psychotherapy effectiveness research. A meta-analytic study by Horvath and Symonds (1991) implies that 26 per cent of the variation in therapeutic success can be attributed to the quality of the alliance. As discussed in the answer to Question 4.3, Cartwright et al. (1996) have explored some of the implications of this for the training, support and effectiveness of counsellors in the alcohol field. Commenting on the results of Project MATCH, Orford points out that 'different forms of individual psychotherapy, provided they are competently delivered by skilled therapists operating in . . . an efficient . . . service delivery organisation . . . are so functionally equivalent that differences between treatments – main or matching – are unlikely' (1999: 64). It is the context and the relationship that emerges as client and therapist work together, which accounts for the success or failure of the therapeutic enterprise.

Concluding observations

- We have lived with alcohol- and drug-related problems for centuries; it is unlikely there are easily identified solutions or 'cures' out there just waiting to be discovered.
- The real-life experiences of drug and alcohol users and the social circumstances that shape their lives powerfully influence their 'success' during and after treatment.
- The users and ex-users of treatment/counselling services should be more actively and imaginatively involved in naturalistic studies to investigate 'what works'.
- Carefully devised research studies bear very little relationship to the many over-stretched drug services, which may employ practitioners with minimal training in addictions counselling.
- The alleviation of the harm and distress of addiction cannot be limited to psychological interventions: clients' material, social and physiological circumstances need to be fully addressed in treatment settings.
- In order to begin to reduce the suspicion that many practitioners have of either using outcome research or contributing to it, education and

training that provides them with a language to articulate what they are doing with their clients, and why, must be given a higher priority.

Rose Kent

* * *

4.3 I would like to be able to offer counselling to addicted clients but I am unsure what qualities a counsellor in this field should possess. I have heard that some counsellors in this field have had personal experiences of addiction in the past. Is this likely to be helpful?

The qualities, experience, training and other characteristics of counsellors that are most helpful to clients have interested theorists and researchers for many years. In the 1950s, with the influence of Carl Rogers and subsequent person-centred approaches, the role and attributes of the therapist were for the first time subject to scientific scrutiny. The 'core conditions' of congruence, acceptance and empathy in the therapist were identified as necessary and sufficient for personal growth to occur in the client. Bergin and Garfield (1994) describe the more recent research evidence, which still tends to support the long-standing view that psychotherapy and counselling are a process of interpersonal persuasion, in which the therapeutic values, beliefs and optimism of the therapist are the most potent ingredients. They serve to 'overcome demoralization, instil hope and provide a believable meaning of life for clients' (Bergin and Garfield 1994).

In researching effective practitioner qualities specifically in the alcohol field, Cartwright et al. (1996) use the term 'therapeutic commitment' to describe three aspects of the practitioner which influence behaviour towards clients with alcohol problems: the therapist's or practitioner's self-esteem when working with such clients, their willingness to do this work, and their expectation of resulting job satisfaction. When these are positive, a good therapeutic alliance is established and therapy is more likely to be effective. Their research indicates that there is a strong association between the therapeutic commitment of the person conducting the assessment interview in a specialist alcohol counselling service, and the likelihood of the client engaging in treatment. The latter is also linked to the client's experience of the interviewer as interpersonally warm. They state that a crucial question for clients seems to be 'How does the worker see me?' Given the low self-esteem of many of clients with addiction problems, it makes sense that this should be of fundamental significance for both their engagement in treatment, and its eventual successful outcome. As well as emphasizing the importance of therapy-specific attributes, which contribute to the effectiveness of the interpersonal process, rather than of broad, inferred 'personality characteristics', Cartwright et al. also emphasize that the attitude of the therapist contributes either to a negative or a positive spiral. Thus, defensiveness or intolerant attitudes in the therapist can destroy any potential or successful outcomes, no matter how skilled he or she may be.

A study by Luborsky et al. (1986) compares three different psychological treatment approaches for opiate users in a methadone maintenance clinic. They attempt to ensure consistency of therapeutic approach by requiring therapists to conform to manual-based therapies, and by selecting very experienced therapists. The three qualities they examine are the therapist's personal adjustment, therapeutic skill and a measure of 'interest in helping patients'. The 'helping alliance' is also measured and this, like therapists' qualities, is found to be moderately related to outcome. The variability of individual therapists – whether or not they are supposedly delivering the same treatment – is also demonstrated by Miller et al. (1980): among nine para-professional therapists, the least effective show a 25 per cent 'success' rate and the most effective 100 per cent – when outcomes for each of their caseloads are averaged. Another study shows about two-thirds of the variance in outcome to be linked to the degree of empathy shown by therapists during treatment (Miller et al. 1980). At 12 months, therapist empathy still accounts for half of the variance in outcomes, and after 24 months a quarter (Miller and Baca 1983).

In a study by Valle (1981) 'interpersonal functioning' (empathy, genuineness, respect and concreteness in the therapeutic interaction) is examined, and it is found that the higher the level of within-session interpersonal functioning by therapists, the less frequent and briefer are the client's relapses. There are marked differences in the effectiveness of the eight counsellors who are taking part.

It appears then that in both the rather limited research in the addictions field, and the more extensive work done in the general psychotherapy field, the ability of the therapist to form a successful therapeutic 'working alliance' with a particular client or client group is crucial. This tends to vary somewhat according to the characteristics of the client, but interpersonal warmth, empathy and openness in the therapist seem to be prerequisites.

With regard to personal experience, research neither supports nor negates the usefulness of addiction counsellors having themselves had alcohol or other drug problems. In practice, there are advantages and disadvantages and much depends on the extent to which individuals have been able to move on from the role of client and have a sense of role legitimacy – i.e. they can identify with the role, tasks and ethics of 'helper/practitioner', whether paid or unpaid. When this involves counselling as an activity, it is crucial that professional boundaries are carefully maintained and differences between counselling and other roles such as sponsor, advocate or befriender are clarified. Possible difficulties include counsellors using their position to work through their own problems vicariously, and having conflicting or unhelpful motives about sharing information about their own life with clients. There can also be the danger of being too self-referential, that is, tending to contribute personal experience or opinion when it is the client's experience or view which should be sought, and his or her uniqueness valued. On the other hand, there are significant advantages in being able to identify with what clients are going through, in having the compassion that comes from having 'been there' oneself, and in being able to act as a role model for clients. Many counsellors who have been through some form of treatment themselves are also particularly skilled at recognizing and challenging therapy 'games'. Overall, there is much to be said for ensuring that staff teams, trainee groups and projects include counsellors from a variety of backgrounds, simply to extend opportunities to learn from one another's experiences.

Rose Kent

* * *

4.4 Is it necessary or advisable to undertake specialist training in order to work effectively with clients having addictive problems? Are there ways in which I could develop my skill in being able to help addicted clients without undergoing lengthy, specialist training?

How these questions are answered depends of course to a large extent on what skills and experience the counsellor already has, and on his or her ability to apply these to a 'different ' client group. As described in Question 4.3 and elsewhere in this book, appropriate attitudes to drug-using clients are crucial, including a positive and optimistic stance, and commitment; and it is unclear whether most types of training courses facilitate the development of such attitudes. Some would argue that specialist training only develops the practitioner's 'role adequacy' – that is, just acquiring knowledge about addiction, its consequences and how it can be overcome – and that unless he or she feels secure in this role, their ability to form effective therapeutic relationships is limited. Role legitimacy and role support matter: that is, being confident that you are entitled to be offering help to the individual with whom you are working, and being in a setting which supports this (Cartwright and Gorman 1993). Training needs to include ways of developing this, as well as supportive supervision and guided practical experience over an extended period of time.

Many addictions counsellors in the United Kingdom have not had specialist training – most rely on a combination of either initial professional training (usually in nursing or social work) or personal experience of overcoming a drug problem, topped up with either short courses in counselling or a counselling qualification. Some will have participated in in-house schemes (such as the Volunteer Alcohol Counsellor Training Scheme, originally validated by Alcohol Concern but now virtually extinct), or *Talking it Through* (Kent 1995), which can be linked to National Vocational Qualifications. There are around 20 specialist courses in the substance misuse field, leading to a recognized qualification, that all include a substantial counselling component. Information about these can be obtained from NAADAC, Alcohol Concern or the policy and practice team at Drugscope. Those qualified counsellors who wish to become familiar with policy, research and practice issues in the 'drugs field' should also contact these organizations for information about other relevant short courses. Conferences are a useful source of knowledge. In addition, some treatment agencies, training organizations and independent trainers run workshops and events on practical skills, such as motivational interviewing and topical issues such as drug use and pregnancy.

In general, the quality of courses varies considerably, particularly with regard to the amount of time and feedback available for skills development. For this reason, before investing considerable time and money, it is often a good idea when applying to ask if you can talk to a previous student on the course.

It is difficult to predict what sort of specialist training in addictions counselling will emerge in the next few years. It is likely to be driven by the development of National Occupational Standards – which are only just being developed – and by the National Treatment Agency – which is in its infancy. The former will describe good practice for workers performing a particular function, will describe the knowledge and skills required and criteria for assessing competence, and will provide the basis for NVQs and SVQs. The Standards will aim to be specific to different types of intervention, organization and focus. It is not yet clear to what extent 'counselling' will be identified as a service delivery function. An advantage of the development of Occupational Standards is that they are not attached to specific qualifications, and also that they should hopefully provide a framework for designing and delivering training programmes.

It may become necessary in the future to undertake specialist training in order to work as a bona fide addictions counsellor within treatment settings that conform to nationally agreed quality standards. In the meantime, interested counsellors may wish to develop a portfolio of evidence that they have attended a variety of conferences, short courses and workshops of different types. It may be possible to set up a supervised placement in an addictions agency, where valuable experience can be gained in a supportive setting. There are also distance learning courses, for instance through the Leeds Addiction Unit, which provide a sound knowledge base. It is best to assume that no single approach or short course will provide sufficient knowledge or skill for a real grasp of working with clients with addictive problems. The confidence, therapeutic commitment and the rewards of this specialism will accumulate gradually but steadily, over a number of years!

Rose Kent

* * *

4.5 When working with clients who also have issues with drugs or alcohol, would it be advisable for me to find a supervisor who specializes in addictions in order to get help about this?

Supervision is an essential element of working in the addictions field, whether one is a specialist or a generic counsellor helping existing clients with their drug or alcohol issues. Many would argue that all counselling should be adequately supervised – but in some settings this is not automatically the case. Some of the reasons for recommending that addictions counselling should only be undertaken if satisfactory supervision arrangements are in place, are listed below:

- Many counsellors feel ill-equipped to tackle addiction problems. Initial training courses are likely to include only a one-day workshop or a few hours' introduction to the topic of substance misuse, addiction and/or alcohol problems. They rarely address the particular skills, attitudes and specialist knowledge or common difficulties that may be encountered in day-to-day work with this client group. For generically trained counsellors, it may be difficult to find suitable courses to fill this gap, whereas good supervision will – over time – do this.

- There are many 'highs and lows' in addictions counselling, seeming sometimes to parallel the drug user's or heavy drinker's life. The counsellor may feel immense optimism or enthusiasm at certain times, with despair or a sense of failure at others. By talking through this in supervision, counsellors are likely to be able to reach a more measured understanding of their experience and be more realistic about the apparently chaotic and unpredictable elements of the counselling work.

- An increasing number of clients with alcohol and other drug problems do not make an independent, active choice to enter counselling. They may be ordered by the court to participate in a treatment or a methadone maintenance programme which includes counselling, or there may be pressure from social services, the criminal justice or education system whereby individuals are led to believe that agreeing to counselling will reduce the threat of further statutory involvement. This is of course linked to the fact that addiction problems frequently impact on the public at large, or significant people in the client's immediate environment, and agents of social control are seeking ways to reduce actual or potential drug-related harm. Whilst many treatment services are used to cooperating with these agencies, their role – and the way one part of the system affects another part – can either undermine the client's progress, or provide encouragement and motivation. The individual counsellor can easily lose sight of these other influences, or become caught up in difficult ethical, bureaucratic or legal complexities if he or she is part of a multi-agency approach. Some counsellors struggle with the moral and/or theoretical issues behind counselling being mandatory. A supervisor who is familiar with these aspects of addictions work will be able to recognize the ethical, practical and systemic aspects of the situation, and support the counsellor in addressing them.

- There are many drug-using clients who have for many years become suspicious of intimate relationships, and relationships with figures of authority. Illegal drug use exists in a world in which trust, consistency and reliability are unfamiliar. Previous treatment experiences may themselves have been unsatisfactory or even punitive. For this reason, establishing a working alliance may be much more demanding and take longer than a generic counsellor would normally expect. A supervisor who is familiar with these challenges can assist the counsellor to develop the necessary patience and skills.

- The majority of counselling for addiction problems occurs within organizations, and supervision by one's line manager is common. While this has some advantages (particularly financial!), there may be important reasons for counsellors to insist on independent, external supervision. There is some evidence (White 1993) that addictions treatment settings are particularly vulnerable to developing unclear boundaries and allowing unethical practice to develop. Of course the majority of organizations try to tackle this at an early stage, but collusion between staff and managers can occur and the individual counsellor is better off having access to a disinterested supervisor who can recognize and assist in dealing with ethical irregularities, if they occur.

Consultancy

An alternative to seeking out an addictions specialist for ongoing supervision is to assess carefully what aspects of the client work one needs support for, and to consult an appropriate person for that purpose. This is perhaps most relevant to experienced counsellors, who are likely to have a number of transferable skills (see also Question 4.4). One example is the competent cognitive-behaviour therapist who feels confident about working with her client on relapse management, but needs to be better informed about alcohol withdrawal symptoms and how long they are likely to last. Another example is an experienced counsellor in a university counselling service who wants support since she works with a young man who wishes to continue recreational drug use but nonetheless appears increasingly dependent on heroin. Whenever there is a felt need for supervision, it is important for practitioners to identify – as far as they are able – what their expectations are, and to ensure there will be a reasonable match between their therapeutic philosophy or model and that of the person they consult.

Rose Kent

* * *

4.6 A client has referred to the 'Twelve Step' approach for addictions. What does this involve, and is such an approach suitable for all addicts?

See the answers to Question 4.7, and in part to Question 3.10.

* * *

4.7 Is there a way of establishing which approach may be most suitable for a particular client?

The way in which this question is phrased is significant. Within some models of intervention within the addictions, it is customary to require that the client should adapt to the requirements of the particular approach that is on offer. Most obviously, the Twelve Step approach is explicit in its attempt to make categorical statements about the nature of addiction, those who are likely to suffer from problems of addiction and the measures that are necessary if 'recovery' is going to be possible (see also Question 3.10). The Twelve Step movement takes its name from the 12 'steps' which are thought to comprise the route to recovery. The 'First Step' within this model is as follows:

> We recognized that we were powerless over alcohol and that our lives had become unmanageable. [With regard to other areas of addiction, the appropriate word is substituted for 'alcohol' as necessary.]

The above 'Step', like those that follow it, and its adoption, is regarded as an essential precursor to the ability to progress sequentially through the remaining Steps. It is of note that this Step (as others) is phrased in the first person plural (i.e. 'we', rather than 'I'), reflecting the importance of the 'addict' being encouraged to surrender aspects of individual differ-ence, and accept instead that he or she must forge a common identity with other 'sufferers' and tread a similar path to recovery. Within this model, individuals who assert that their circumstances are different to those of others may be regarded as 'suffering from terminal uniqueness' – the suggestion is that the very idea of being significantly different is symp-tomatic of the illness from which he or she suffers and will prove unhelp-ful.

Within models closely allied to disease theories of addiction, the approach is one that requires the individual to identify with and conform to the beliefs and value-systems of the model. There are easy parallels here with the medical paradigm in which orthodox medicine diagnoses the nature of illness and prescribes the appropriate treatment. It is the patient's role to cooperate with the treatment that has been prescribed.

The question asked here, however, requires us to think of a process by which intervention may be tailored to the need of particular individuals. Rather than suggesting that there is one approach which is necessary for all, we are asked to consider the possibility that each individual may require a unique approach, although almost inevitably there is much common ground in terms of what may prove useful to many. Even within the 'Twelve Step Facilitation', counsellors inevitably modify their approaches in order to respond to the circumstances of particular clients (Project MATCH 1997).

The approach that a counsellor offers to a particular client is to some degree inevitably idiosyncratic. The counsellor's personality, theoretical preferences, current supervision arrangements, training and so on are expressed in the way in which he or she perceives and responds to a given client. It is perhaps one of the most important competences of counsellors that they are able to integrate such dispositional factors with an attuned response to the needs of the particular client with whom they may be working. Experience and intuition are very important factors in assisting the ability to achieve such an integration.

It may be helpful to describe a means by which counsellor and client can work together to construct a 'Drug-taking Hypothesis' – a framework for understanding the way in which a client has come to use drugs, the difficulties that arise as a result of drug use, and ways in which these difficulties might be successfully addressed (Cartwright et al. 1997).

The 'Drug-taking Hypothesis' comprises several interlinked elements, as follows:

- the pattern of drug use
- the reasons for drug use
- the harm resulting from drug use
- specific vulnerability factors
- degree of physical addiction
- the client's preferred explanatory model.

Pattern of drug use

An understanding of the client's pattern of drug use needs to encompass three elements – quantity, quality, and frequency of use:

1. Quantity of use: the extent of most drug-related problems is directly related to the quantity of drugs consumed.
2. Quality of drugs used: differing preparations of the same drug may have widely differing strengths. Although alcohol has the same chemical composition in both beer and spirits, the respective strengths of these beverages is clearly very different. Illegally supplied drugs are also likely to vary tremendously in strength. Two batches of heroin purchased from the same dealer within a short space of time may differ tremendously in potency and/or purity. It is often argued that the illegality of certain drugs removes them from any effective means of quality control, thus leading to sometimes dangerous variations in the quality and strength of drugs which are consumed.
3. Frequency/variability of drug use: some drugs are extremely unlikely to cause problems if used very infrequently, whereas others represent a significant risk each time the drug is taken. An understanding of the frequency of drug use and the factors that determine this frequency forms a vital part in understanding the overall way in which a client uses drugs. Some people report that they use drugs only at certain times or in particular circumstances. Once again, an understanding of the factors that influence the variability of use can be very helpful in comprehending the wider picture.

The reasons for drug use

A detailed model for understanding reasons for drug use is given in the answer to Question 2.1. That model is fairly functional in its emphasis, and it can be very helpful to supplement it with an empathic understanding of the 'relationship' that the client enjoys with the drug(s) of choice. For example, the client very often manifests a persisting affectional bond to the drug, which is not necessarily reduced by the acknowledgement that the same drug causes difficulty (Jackson 2001; Reading 2001).

The harm resulting from drug use

It is helpful not only to identify the fact that drug use causes some form of harm to the client, but also to examine the particular ways in which drug use gives rise to such harm, as outlined in the answer to Question 2.2. Differing modes of intervention vary in their approach to the reduction of drug-related harms (Keene 1997).

Specific vulnerability factors

The assessment of the vulnerability of a particular client is essentially a means of understanding why it is that this particular client has been disposed to suffer a particular form of harm, and whether the disposition to experience harm is likely to continue in the future if drugs continue to be consumed. Identification of such areas of vulnerability makes it possible to consider ways in which the client can be helped not only to address current difficulties, but also to minimize the risks of relapse in the future (see Question 5.6). Such vulnerabilities may represent unresolved areas of need to which drug use has been a response in the past. For example, the client who lacks a viable sense of personal identity may be assisted in developing a more robust self-image through counselling. A failure to attend to this 'vulnerability' makes it more likely that drugs will be used for similar purposes in the future. (Even apparently 'negative' identities such as 'addict', 'druggie' or 'alcoholic' may seem preferable to none at all.)

Degree of physical addiction

The use of drugs in order to relieve or prevent the occurrence of withdrawal symptoms can represent the single most important factor in constructing the drug-taking hypothesis. Under such circumstances, the counsellor may be best advised to direct initial efforts towards assisting the client in finding ways to break the 'addictive cycle' which he or she may have established (see Question 3.7).

Although the effects of withdrawal symptoms and associated 'relief drug use' can be very profound, clients often have a very poor understanding of what is going on. The client's improved understanding of such matters can provide tremendous relief, particularly in helping to understand better some of the more difficult experiences which may have occurred. The client who is able to see that much past behaviour can be best understood in the context of an escalating physical addiction to a drug may be helped to feel less guilty, crazy, and so on, and more able to take effective action to bring about change. The client's ability to appreciate the influence of 'physical addiction' is often much improved after he or she has been able to 'break the cycle'. Thus, the counsellor's ability to 'hold' an understanding of what is happening at such times becomes particularly important whilst the client develops the ability to reflect more fully on what has been happening.

The client's preferred explanatory model

Clients vary in the ways in which they describe their relationships with drugs. While few clients employ formal, psychological language, the counsellor can nevertheless attend sensitively to the way in which the client articulates his or her difficulties. An understanding gained in this way can assist the counsellor in deciding which approaches might be more suitable for each particular client (see Figure 4.1). For example, some clients may speak of the difficulties they are having in terms that are very compatible with the belief system central to disease models of addiction. A client who reports that drug use is driven by forces that seem beyond conscious control, and who is unable to imagine any way by which more controlled use might be achieved, may be quite suited to the Twelve Step programmes and/or interventions that are compatible with these. On the other hand, a client who reports significant links between

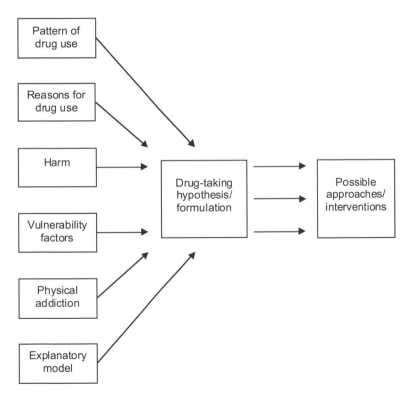

Figure 4.1. Using the drug-taking hypothesis to generate possible therapeutic approaches/interventions.

excessive drug use and particular life difficulties may benefit from an approach that addresses such difficulties and that places relatively little emphasis upon the use of drugs per se.

The more that the counsellor can empathize with the way in which the client tends to experience his or her relationship with drugs, the more it becomes possible to employ language and metaphors that have resonance with the client's experience. In turn, the ability to discuss the client's drug use in such a way provides a bridge to drawing on those aspects of theory and intervention that are likely to have most validity for the client.

Differing aspects of the hypothesis may be couched in quite different terms and suggest that interventions from various perspectives can be usefully combined. For example, a client may be using drugs in order to address several simultaneous areas of need. Drug use may be required in order to avoid withdrawal symptoms, to 'self-medicate' because of distress arising from early experience, to maintain the homeostasis of a family system, and to cope with situations in which no other coping response seems to be available. This example appears to indicate the possibility of combining interventions from medicine, dynamic psychotherapy, systemic family therapy and behavioural self-control training.

There are times when the counsellor regards the client's 'preferred explanatory model' as one that limits rather than increases the potential for change. The client who asserts that drug use is a matter that is beyond his or her control may be operating from a belief system that reduces the potential to acknowledge the sense of agency and choice in determining the quality of future drug use. Under such circumstances, the counsellor should work towards a mutual understanding that the current approach is unhelpful, and seek to collaborate with the client in developing a hypothesis that is more conducive to the possibility of change. Clearly any formulation that is generated needs to be flexible and adaptable as new material and understanding evolves.

Bill Reading

* * *

4.8 How can I tell if someone may need specialist help for his or her drug use?

Many people use drugs or alcohol recreationally without developing serious problems that require specialist help. On the other hand, those people who do have problems because of the use of drugs or alcohol often do not seek help; or they come to the notice of appropriate services only when their problems are advanced. In general, the earlier that problems are acknowledged and help is sought, the better the prospects are for a successful resolution. If you suspect that someone may have problems with drugs or alcohol, it is best to seek appropriate professional advice about this as early as possible.

It is also important to realize that 'addiction' is not a unitary phenomenon with any single measure of severity. It is possible for someone to develop medical, social or psychological problems as a result of drugs or alcohol without being 'dependent', or even in the case of alcohol without drinking more than the recommended 'safe' limits. It is also possible, for example, for people to be physically dependent on opiates without developing serious problems in other areas of their lives.

In general, however, if someone has symptoms of neuro-adaptation, or physical dependence on drugs or alcohol (see Question 2.7), with evidence of tolerance to the effects of the substance taken and withdrawal symptoms, then they are likely to need specialist help. Similarly, if they continue to take drugs or alcohol in spite of an awareness of the physical, psychological or social problems that result, then specialist advice should be considered.

It is not unusual for people to seek counselling or psychotherapy for life problems or for symptoms where substance misuse, particularly alcohol abuse, plays a major role in the origin or perpetuation of their problems. They are, however, often not aware of this or willing to acknowledge it.

Physical or medical problems due to substance misuse may develop and reach an advanced stage quite unknown to the person involved, and not detectable by anyone else except through special investigations: for example, hypertension or liver failure with alcohol, or hepatitis or HIV infection with intravenous drug use. If a person admits to excessive alcohol consumption or a history of drug use by injection during the course of counselling or psychotherapy, the possibility of physical assessment needs be considered. This is especially so if the patient has gastro-intestinal symptoms (such as indigestion, jaundice, abdominal swelling and so on) or neurological symptoms (such as confusion or forgetfulness, loss of sensation, muscular weakness or lack of coordination), or any other unexplained medical symptoms.

Psychological problems due to drugs or alcohol are common and the underlying cause is often missed. Anyone being treated for anxiety or depression in whom drug or alcohol use is discovered should be carefully re-evaluated, with specialist assessment or re-assessment if necessary. In general, it is not possible to make a clinical diagnosis of anxiety disorder or of depressive illness unless the person has been substance-free for several weeks and is still symptomatic. More serious psychiatric illnesses, such as psychosis, may also be caused or exacerbated by drugs or alcohol.

Similarly, social problems are particularly common in drug or alcohol abuse, and the link between the substance misuse and the problem may not always be made by the professionals involved. Problems at work, including absenteeism, deteriorating performance or accidents may occur. Problems in relationships are common, including arguments, violence, jealousy or sexual difficulties; and substance misuse is often implicated in the sexual or physical abuse of children or in child neglect. Criminal activity may be engaged in, either as a result of disinhibition, or to obtain funds for substance misuse.

A person may lose interest in their normal activities and relationships, as substance misuse becomes more and more central to their lives. Eventually, much of the person's time and energy is spent in acquiring, consuming or recovering from the effects of the desired substance.

In general, the counsellor should be as open as possible with the client about the possible role of substance misuse in his or her life and the links with any specific problems identified. The need for further specialist assessment or treatment should be raised and ways of obtaining this explored. If counsellors are working in a medical setting, they may seek permission to discuss these issues, or to make a referral to the GP or to local specialist services. Alternatively, it may be possible to consult with local specialist services, many of which offer such advice and support to professionals, either with the client's permission or without giving identifying details.

In more general terms, it is sensible to familiarize oneself with local specialist services, how to contact them and whether they offer consultation. It may also be appropriate to get to know local GPs and find out how to liaise with them should the need arise, even if not working in a medical setting. It may also be worth attending brief training events aimed at recognizing and assessing addiction problems, or about counselling patients with such problems. Substance misuse problems are common. If they are at all significant, they can cause serious difficulties in counselling or psychotherapy if not detected or addressed effectively.

Bill Plummer

CHAPTER 5

Motivational enhancement and relapse prevention

5.1 Is it true that people cannot be helped to change unless they really admit that they have a problem?

Over the past 20 years in particular, the whole understanding of 'change' in the addictions field has evolved creatively. Most obviously this relates to the conceptual framework offered by social learning models, out of which emerged the therapeutic approach known as motivational interviewing (Miller 1983), allied to the transtheoretical model of change (Prochaska and Diclemente 1986). Whilst these constructs are no longer accepted unequivocally, their influence in both theory and practice cannot be underestimated. Current thinking is captured succinctly in Heather's observation that 'addictive disorders are essentially motivational problems' (1992).

Historical perspective

The perceived lack of motivation to change in those clients who misuse substances was historically attributed to the pernicious nature of the disorder. This resulted in supposed personality traits that manifested themselves in the client's 'denial', 'resistance' and absence of motivation. Within this model of understanding, successful treatment was contingent upon the client eventually accepting the reality and severity of his or her problem in the face of irrefutable evidence, out of which there then emerged the motivation to change. The work of treatment agencies was to toil away, endlessly confronting the client's defences until they finally 'broke'. The nature of this approach is captured in Nace's statement that 'the effective resolution of pathological denial is the *sine qua non* of alcoholism treatment' (1987). There are clear lines of demarcation here whereby failures of treatment are due to the client's deficits whereas successes are testament to the quality of treatments offered. Significantly, no evidence has ever emerged that suggests any of the above qualities are personality traits specific to this client group, although this perception remains imbued in the folklore of many treatment agencies and in much of society as a whole. However, it also needs to be acknowledged that some clients both prefer and respond well to this approach, considering it to fit better with how they experience their own substance use. Equally, others respond well to simply being advised where they are going wrong and what to do about it, by someone they consider has the knowledge and authority to do this. This is understandable if attributions such as 'Alcoholism is the only disease that tells you "You don't have a problem"' are held as true; and it again illustrates the client's right to choose which approach intuitively feels most appropriate for him or her.

Change as a process

Emerging out of clinical experience, Miller (1983) proposed an alternative model, which suggested that denial is not an inherent trait but is rather the product of how counsellors choose to interact with substance misusers. This denial was exacerbated by the belief that the only possible treatment approach was complete and lifelong abstinence. Miller illustrates this with the example of a person in two minds about his drinking. On one hand, the client recognizes some problems emerging, but on the other hand still enjoys aspects of his alcohol use and does not want to give up completely. If told that abstinence is the only viable solution, the client is extremely likely to produce a counter argument. The counsellor interprets this as 'denial' and confronts this forcibly. The client will equally forcibly try to preserve his or her position. Unwittingly, the counsellor's approach to the problem has elicited this response in the client. The principles of social psychology demonstrate that direct argumentation is the worst way to try to change the views of another person. The adage of 'I learn what I believe as I hear myself talk' ensures that the more a person verbally defends a position, the more committed the person becomes to it.

It can be seen therefore that change and motivation to change is not an 'either/or state', but rather a shifting, dynamic process. This is the case both in terms of how clients experience themselves, and how this experience is responded to by others. In this context, it is not necessary for clients to 'really admit' they have a problem, although many do this of their own volition. Instead a viable starting point is the acknowledgement that they have *some concerns* related to aspects of their substance use. Miller suggests specific interventions, which are described in the answers to Questions 5.2, 5.3 and 5.4. However, it is clear that non-confrontational, empathic, person-centred counsellor approaches are eminently appropriate in addressing these areas of change or possible change with the client. A practical working definition has been arrived at that describes motivation as the 'probability that a person will enter into, continue and adhere to a specific change process' (Miller 1985).

The nature of ambivalence

Ambivalence around change is now better understood not as the manifestation of an underlying pathological denial but as a normal human experience. Working with the client's experience of ambivalence is seen as central to enhancing motivation to change. It is noted by Davidson (1996) that the understanding of ambivalence has a long history in both analytic and cognitive/behavioural literature. As far back as 1911, Bleuler suggested three types:

1. Voluntary ambivalence – a conscious conflict about doing one thing versus another
2. Intellectual ambivalence – a simultaneous interpretation of experience in positive and negative ways
3. Emotional ambivalence – refers specifically to the feelings of love and hate directed to the same object.

Another conceptualization of ambivalence from a cognitive/behavioural perspective seems particularly apposite when considering substance misuse:

1. Approach–Approach conflict. The person has to choose between two equally attractive alternatives, with the important choice factors being positive.
2. Avoidance–Avoidance conflict. The person has to choose between two equally negative alternatives.
3. Approach–Avoidance conflict. The person has to choose between a single object he is both attracted to and repelled by. This is characterized by the person alternating between gratifying and resisting the behaviour.

It is vital to acknowledge that the subjective experience of ambivalence can be extremely unpleasant, particularly if the client feels stuck and unable to initiate a course of action that would resolve the conflict. Ellis et al. (1988) describe this dilemma eloquently in the context of substance misuse when they observe: 'The reason addictions are too easy to create and maintain is that no cognitive or behavioural strategy can eliminate the discomfort anxiety as quickly and as effortlessly as chemicals.'

Change and loss

Broadly speaking, the client's relationship with substances is conceptualized in terms of how it is used intra- and interpersonally, and how adaptational factors such as tolerance develop over time due to the intrinsic pharmacological effects of the substances taken. Great care is taken when considering making change to explore what the absence of the above factors might mean for the client, both from a positive and negative perspective. However, the actual 'nature' of the client's relationship with substances is sometimes extremely powerful and far greater than the sum of its parts. To use an analogy, a person can describe specific qualities in someone they love, but this does not adequately account for why they love these qualities, or the person. Neither does it convey what this experience truly feels like, as it is perhaps beyond words and can only be 'experienced'. A significant number of clients have these feelings about the substances they use, and even when motivated to change, the anticipated loss can be unimaginable. These relationships are most readily understood through the principles of Attachment Theory, where an attachment bond is described as 'a special form of relationship that is characterised by feelings of comfort when near the other person and a desire to remain close when distressed or when this person is inaccessible' (Ball and Legow 1996).

Considering this statement in terms of a how a client experiences their relationship with drink or drugs, and how this might be usefully responded to, can be very facilitative. Reading (2001) has offered a conceptualization that brings these ideas more specifically into the therapy of the addictions. Furthermore, addressing these areas also falls readily under the remit of general counselling approaches, as understanding some clients' relationships with substances requires an emotive, feeling language and engagement, into which social learning and associated cognitive behavioural models cannot easily enter (Jackson 2001). For those clients who do relate in this way to the substances they use, change is more likely to be facilitated if the counsellor is able to work in a genuine, sensitive manner with the intrinsic quality of this relationship.

Counsellor factors

It is generally considered that clients seen by reflective, understanding and empathic counsellors are more likely to resolve their ambivalence, and that from this their motivation to change is also more likely to emerge (Davidson 1996). An important part of this understanding is the acceptance that the client is frequently likely to change his or her position, often within the same session, so that the counsellor needs to guard against becoming preoccupied with the outcome; instead the counsellor needs to remain empathic to the client's struggle. Equally, the counsellor needs to remember that the pace of change is set by the client, and that the client will decide what does, or does not, constitute something he or she wishes to change. This can be an extremely frustrating process for counsellors, when they see clients doing something that, from the counsellors' perspective, seems very damaging and well within the clients' abilities to address. Here the temptation is often to subtly manoeuvre the agenda and covertly 'persuade' the client to change; but in all probability the client will just as subtly resist this. In this context, Rogers' (1987) dictum that 'people are most likely to change when they feel free not to' is particularly instructive.

Paul Jackson

* * *

5.2 What can the counsellor do to encourage the client to actually make changes in his or her use of drink or drugs?

As discussed in relation to Question 5.1, change is most usefully understood and responded to as a shifting, dynamic process. The movements from 'contemplating' change, through the decisional point of 'determination' into 'action', are stages where the incorporation of motivational techniques are considered particularly helpful. These 'stages' are expanded upon in the answer to Question 5.3, within the overall context of Prochaska and Diclemente's transtheoretical model of change (1986). More recently, motivational interviewing skills have been incorporated into an overall model known as motivational enhancement therapy. The focus in this answer is on specific interventions: a fuller exposition of this is in Miller and Rollnick's *Motivational Interviewing: Preparing People to Change Addictive Behaviours* (1991).

Motivational factors in the therapeutic relationship

Emphasis on the nature and quality of the therapeutic relationship has increased awareness of what a potent agent of change this relationship is in itself. In turn, this means that therapy in the field of substance misuse is increasingly grounded in the context of this relationship, which helps reduce the perception of it as an area of clinical specialism. Saunders et al. (1991) suggest in that 'in essence [motivational enhancement therapy] is nothing more than the application of good counselling skills to the addictions area'. Elaborating upon this, Jackson (2000a) suggests three motivation-enhancing factors that may emerge naturally out of a healthy therapeutic relationship:

1. If the counsellor is warm, empathic and accepting, the more negative view clients have of themselves is challenged, and their sense of self-esteem and efficacy might naturally be strengthened. In turn, this increases the quality of the therapeutic alliance, which also enhances the likelihood of healthy change.
2. Working in this way helps in facilitating a deeper understanding of the client's relationship with the substance he or she uses, as opposed to remaining solely at the more surface level of 'how' the substance is misused.
3. Entering unconditionally and empathically into the client's relationship with substances is likely to encourage the finding of words that helps the client usefully articulate any ambivalence around possible change.

The nature of growth and change

The foundation of Miller's original formulation of motivational interviewing (1983) is the belief, taken from humanistic psychology, in the 'individual's inherent wisdom and ability to choose the healthful path given sufficient support'. By definition, therefore, the client already has a predisposed drive to seek accomplishment of innate potential; and the counsellor's task is to try to provide an atmosphere and environment that enhances this natural drive. Individual counsellors obviously need to consider their own position in relation to this conceptualization of human nature, both in terms of their personal philosophy, and the integration of motivational techniques into their existing practice.

Principles of motivational enhancement

Miller and Rollnick (1991) outline five broad clinical principles that underlie and inform all their motivational interventions.

Express empathy

This is presented in the context of Rogerian, person-centred philosophy, and refers both to a general counsellor presence characterized by warmth and acceptance, and to the allied use of counsellor skills such as reflective listening, open questions, summarizing, etc.

Develop discrepancy

The aim is to create and expand, in the client's mind, a discrepancy between present behaviour and broader goals: i.e. facilitating the client's awareness of the gap between where the client is now, and where he or she wants to be. Therefore, when a certain behaviour is experienced as conflicting with important personal goals, beliefs or values, often related to health, happiness and/or self-image, then change is likely to occur, in order to reduce the 'dissonance' that comes with holding such discrepant views. The following example from Premack (1970) illustrates this process. He describes a situation in which a man was due to pick up his children from the library. A thunderstorm greeted his arrival, while at the same time he realized he was out of cigarettes. He caught a glimpse of his children emerging out into the downpour, but carried on driving, hopeful he could park quickly, buy some cigarettes and be back before they got seriously wet. He found humiliating this view of himself as a father who would leave his children to get soaked while he hunted for cigarettes, and at that point quit smoking. Once into awareness, his behaviour was experienced as discrepant with how he wanted to perceive himself as a father. The ensuing discomfort provided the motivation for change; stopping smoking restored a positive sense of himself.

Obviously these interactions, to a lesser or greater extent, are occurring all the time within the normal vagaries of life, often not coming into consciousness, or being resolved without requiring conscious consideration. Clearly therapy cannot 'arrange' their happening. However, motivational interventions seek to enhance and amplify what is there, until it overrides attachment to the current behaviour. It is important that this is sought 'within' the person, rather than relying upon external factors (such as family pressure), which are felt as more coercive. Central to this approach is facilitating clients' presentations of their personal reasons for change, rather than others' ideas as to why they should change, although it needs to be recognized that the latter are invariably a starting point in the early stages of counselling.

Avoid argumentation

The counsellor is active in avoiding arguments and interpersonal confrontation. The worst possible scenario, as discussed in the answer to Question 5.1, is where the counsellor attempts to convince the client of his or her problem and need to change, whilst the client defends the opposite position. However, motivational enhancement is confrontational in its stated purpose, to promote awareness of difficulties and facilitate the likelihood of change, but in a gently persuasive style that has been described as 'soft confrontation' (Miller and Rollnick, 1991).

Four categories of resistant behaviour have been identified:

1. Arguing – the client contests the accuracy, skill, knowledge or integrity of the counsellor.
2. Interrupting – the client breaks in and interrupts in a defensive manner.
3. Denying – the client demonstrates an unwillingness to recognize problems, cooperate, accept responsibility or consider advice offered.
4. Ignoring – the client shows evidence of not following or ignoring the counsellor.

In this context, client resistance or reluctance is not seen as something to break through, but rather an indication to the counsellor that a different intervention or approach is required to restore the therapeutic alliance. Again, this is based on the premise of starting with the client at the point where he or she is, and remaining guided by the client throughout the process.

Roll with resistance

Allied to the above, although neither arguing nor confronting, the counsellor is nonetheless active in working with the content of the client's statements. The momentum generated by the client's words is not blocked, but slightly reframed or reflected, thus directing this momentum more towards change. Miller and Rollnick (1991) states this is only help-ful in the counsellor's complete acceptance of the client's personal responsibility. It is the client's decision what to do about a difficulty; this is in the belief that the client is capable, and in possession of insights and ideas for the resolution of his or her own problems. Therefore, goals and answers are not imposed. Instead, clients are invited to consider new information in the light of differing perspectives, and encouraged to generate their own possible solutions. In particular, interventions at these times consist largely of reflecting, amplified reflection, double-sided reflection (acknowledging and affirming what the client has said, whilst adding to it the other side of ambivalence expressed), reframing and emphasizing personal choice and control. As stated elsewhere, it can be seen that these are very much general counselling approaches and skills that fit readily within most models.

Support self-efficacy

In general, self-efficacy refers to a person's belief in his or her ability to carry out and succeed with a specific task. Self-efficacy is presented as a key element in motivation to change, but is perhaps better seen as *the key* element if change is to actually take place. Recognizing a difficulty gets the client no further, unless the client has belief in his or her ability to instigate change. A central tenet of motivational enhancement is in the aim of increasing the client's perceptions of his or her capability both to cope with obstacles, and to succeed with change. Allied to this, of course, is the client's self-esteem, because generally the better the client's sense of self, the better will be his or her self-efficacy. However, this is not always the case, as clients with low self-esteem still make significant change. Esteem often improves in response to changes made – there is now some-thing 'real' to feel better about. All the approaches within motivational enhancement therapy support self-efficacy, as each requires that the client takes personal responsibility. In this way, the counsellor cannot make the change for the client and the client cannot change to please the counsellor. As Miller and Rollnick (1991) succinctly observes: 'The person not only can but must make the change, in the sense that no one else can do it for him or her.'

Paul Jackson

* * *

5.3 Does change tend to occur fairly spontaneously once the client has acknowledged that there may be a need to change?

Conceptualizing the nature of change within the addictions field has been understood over the past 15 years in particular within the framework of Prochaska and Diclemente's 'transtheoretical approach' (1992), more commonly known as the 'model of change' (1986). The model attempts to identify those change factors that are common to all therapeutic approaches, out of which a more integrated response can be developed. The stages of change, which are only part of the model, are often referred to, but this is overly simplistic and the whole approach needs to be considered in the context of all its component parts: each part exists only in relation to another and cannot be understood in isolation. Here I give only a brief overview of the model, but the reader can refer to Prochaska and Diclemente (1986, 1992) for a comprehensive account; to Sutton (1996) for a critical appraisal of its efficacy; and to Jackson (2000b) for a concise presentation of the approach. The model is concerned with how change can best be understood and facilitated, rather than emphasizing the origin of the difficulty. Being transtheoretical, the language used in the model is mostly behavioural in its description, which may at times jar with the reader familiar with exploring these issues from different perspectives.

Basic assumptions

1. The model recognizes, addresses and learns from the observation that many, perhaps most, people make healthy changes in response to life difficulties without ever seeking formal help.
2. The model is equally applicable to the many and varied ways help is offered, from maximum to minimal interventions.
3. The model is an aid to integrating the wide range of therapeutic approaches.
4. The model is applicable to all presenting difficulties. It advances understanding of change in the light of such differing presentations, and seeks to establish commonalties of change, which may help in explaining success or failure in a person's attempt to address his or her difficulties.
5. The model encompasses the full course of change, from becoming aware of the difficulty to the point of resolution.

The model seeks to integrate and apply therapeutically the *processes* of change, according to the identified problem *level*, at specific established *stages* of change.

The processes of change

A process of change represents a form of overt or covert intervention, which is either experienced or initiated by the person in addressing thoughts, feelings and/or behaviours, relative to his or her presenting difficulties. Ten change processes have been identified. Significantly, it has been found that self-changers use the full range of these processes, whereas most systems of therapy use less, due to the restrictions of their specific therapeutic approaches. The ten processes are:

1. Consciousness raising – increasing information about oneself and the problem.
2. Self-liberation – choice, commitment, self-efficacy.
3. Social liberation – increasing alternatives for 'non-problem' behaviour in a societal environment.
4. Counter-conditioning – developing alternatives to the problem behaviours.
5. Stimulus control – avoiding or resisting stimuli that precipitate problem behaviours.
6. Self re-evaluation – reviewing and revising self-perception in relation to the difficulty.
7. Environmental re-evaluation – reviewing how one's difficulties affect, and are affected by, the immediate and wider physical environment.
8. Contingency/reinforcement management – rewarding oneself, or being rewarded, for making change.
9. Dramatic relief – expressing and experiencing feelings relating to both the difficulties and solutions.
10. Helping relationships – being open and trusting about difficulties with those who care and can help.

Levels of change

This represents, in hierarchical order, the five discrete, but nonetheless interrelated, levels of psychological functioning at which interventions may be made:

Level 1. Symptom/situational – the presenting difficulties.

Level 2. Maladaptive cognitions – unhelpful thought patterns and beliefs.

Level 3. Interpersonal conflicts – relationship difficulties in the broadest sense.

Level 4. Family/system conflicts – difficulties specific to immediate family/system.

Level 5. Intrapersonal conflicts – difficulties within the self.

Change initiated at one level is likely to increase the chances of change at another. As an example, a client that reduces his drinking (level 1) is likely to start perceiving things in a more optimistic way (level 2), which in turn may prompt change, or at least re-evaluation, in levels 3, 4 and 5. Although these levels are presented in a hierarchical fashion, this is not prescriptive and the point of intervention is usually at that level that is defined by the client. In practice, these levels are better understood as pragmatic rather than hierarchical, as level 1, the presenting difficulty, is likely to be the most pressing concern for both client and counsellor initially.

Stages of change

While this particular component of the model has been subject to many interpretations and refinements, as a baseline, change is conceptualized as a process that involves moving from, and through, the stages of:

- pre-contemplation
- contemplation
- determination
- action
- maintenance.

Pre-contemplation

The person is not aware of, or more often unable/unwilling to acknowledge, his or her difficulties. This is most often due to factors such as attachment to the behaviour, ambivalence, rationalization and lack of knowledge. At this stage difficulties are frequently obvious to others, who can see what the person has to struggle to acknowledge.

Contemplation

The person begins to explore the possibility of some problem existing, gives thought to what this may be, and considers making change.

Determination

This is conceptualized as something of a fleeting stage, which Miller and Rollnick (1991) call the 'window of opportunity', where the person *resolves* to do something about his or her identified difficulty.

Action

The person has carried through their resolve and is now implementing their own intervention plan.

Maintenance

The person has initiated the proposed change and is now developing ways of consolidating and maintaining these changes.

Whether or not *relapse*, a common enough event in itself, constitutes a stage is something of a moot point. One view suggests relapse is seen only as the medium or event that moves the person back to another, previous stage. The alternative view does not disagree with this, but adds that as relapse is a common occurrence, it should also be included as a distinct stage and normalized within the cycle of change.

Change in practice

In practice of course, change is rarely a smooth, linear process, and this model is often presented as a circular, revolving door or 'spiralling out' concept. This accommodates the reality of clients going round the cycle by 'relapsing' back into old behaviours, and reverting to a previous stage – for example, action to contemplation – and then at some point moving on to the action stage again, via determination. Equally, there is no sense of time, in that clients can remain in a particular stage for a considerable period, or may move swiftly through. The one caveat here is the point of 'determination', which, as described above, is often fleeting, and if not acted upon is often resolved by a return to contemplation. This point of determination can be experienced as extremely uncomfortable by the client and understandably unsustainable in itself, and is only ameliorated as a 'feeling' state either by making a change, or by the decision not to change. It is vital that the counsellor is sensitive to, and empathic with, this struggle.

Clients also present at very different stages, having gone through more or less change themselves prior to seeking outside help. Much of this is of course defined by the nature of different helping agencies and modes of referral. A client seeking therapy, which he or she is happy to fund personally, is likely to be at the contemplation, determination or action stage, whereas the client having to seek help as part of a court order is probably at the pre-contemplation stage.

In conceptualizing this process in practice as a 'cycle' of change, it is observed that clients tend to move in and out of different stages, and through the cycle as a whole several times, before establishing long-term maintenance. In theory, this maintenance stage can be exited from by moving on to a life free from the original difficulty. This is demonstrated in the example given by Prochaska and Diclemente (1986) of successful ex-smokers, who tend to make on average three revolutions through the cycle before exiting totally as non-smokers.

Therapeutic interventions

The following three factors are considered crucial in the context of the model of change:

1. As always the counsellor's first task is to engender a therapeutic relationship grounded in respect, trust and understanding, which supports the client in attempting change.
2. The counsellor is required to approach the task of change systematically, while integrating a wide range of skills and interventions (processes) specific to the needs of each individual client. This is elaborated upon in Question 5.4.
3. The counsellor needs to establish what *stage* the client is at and identify the *level* at which to intervene with the most appropriate intervention *process* (again, see Question 5.4).

It has been suggested that the model of change has an 'intuitive' appeal to practitioners, most obviously because it appears to account for the complexities of change, and to offer ways in which interventions may be most usefully tailored in response to the specific needs of the individual client. However, the transtheoretical nature of this concept also makes great demands of counsellors in terms of how the construct is integrated into existing approaches. In noting that 'self-changers' generally utilize all change processes, whereas therapeutic approaches use less, Prochaska and Diclemente (1992) state unequivocally that therapists should be at least as creative and complex as their clients.

Paul Jackson

* * *

5.4 Should the counsellor adapt his or her approach according to which stage of change the client is in at a particular point in time?

Since the answer to this question involves the 'model of change', the starting point is the answer to Question 5.3, which provides the content for this question. Appreciation of the model of change in helping agencies has increased responses that reflect the individual presentation of each client. Accordingly, interventions (processes) can be facilitated, in partnership with the client, that are both at the correct level and appropriate to his or her stage of change. The simple, common sense of this is undeniable and accounts perhaps for its 'intuitive' appeal. However, the model itself is not simple and makes great demands of the counsellor. Prochaska and Diclemente (1992) caution against what they term 'reductionism for the sake of accessibility', stating that the complexities of change necessitate a multifaceted response.

Matching response to level

Certain broad categories of response are more usual at certain levels, although they are by no means static, since different levels can be addressed concurrently:

Level 1. The presenting difficulty: respond with practical, behavioural, 'doing' strategies.

Level 2. Maladaptive cognitions: respond with approaches that address these thought patterns and beliefs directly.

Level 3. Current interpersonal conflicts: respond with more systemic-based interventions that consider the wider context.

Level 4. Family/system conflicts: as with level 3, more systemic-based interventions.

Level 5. Intrapersonal conflicts: respond with more personal, depth-based counselling in consideration of the 'self'.

Matching response to stage of change

It is in matching the response to the client's identified stage of change that the model is felt to be most clinically useful.

Pre-contemplation

At this stage, the client is not thinking about changing the behaviour and, generally, is attending a helping agency in response to external pressures. Diclemente (1991) summarizes the reasons why people are at this stage, and identifies useful responses to each of the four reasons, the 'four Rs' of reluctance, rebellion, resignation and rationalization:

1. Reluctance is due to lack of knowledge, information or inertia, where the impact of the problem has not become conscious. 'Why change if I don't have a problem?' Useful responses include *empathizing* with the client's situation and experience of himself or herself, and sensitively offering *information* and *feedback*, not necessarily for use now, but to sow seeds for later.
2. Rebellion is due to the client's heavy investment in the problem behaviour, so that he or she often appears hostile to any notion of change. *Respond empathically* to the client's expressed feelings and the conflict that clients find themselves in. *Provide choices* for clients to consider if they want to, in their own time, at their own pace.
3. Resignation is characterized by lack of energy and investment, feeling overwhelmed by the problem and having given up on the possibility of making change. *Respond empathically* to the client's feeling state, tentatively *explore perceived barriers* to change and gently encourage the *instillation of hope*.
4. Rationalization is when clients are not considering change because they actively create plausible reasons as to why it is not a problem for them – for others maybe, but not for them. *Empathizing* with the client's felt dilemma, straightforward *reflective listening* and actively *avoiding argumentation* are helpful interventions.

Three more general points are important to consider when working with clients at this stage:

1. Differentiating between a 'reason' and a 'rationalization' is often unclear. A client can be very aware of the damaging effects of a certain behaviour, but nevertheless make an informed choice to continue with it, based on what for him or her are clear reasons. Not to interpret this as rationalization can obviously be difficult for the counsellor, particularly when the behaviour seems patently self-destructive.
2. Allied to this is the assumption that the problem means the same thing to the client as it does to the counsellor. It is incumbent upon the client to define the problem.
3. The nature of the client's presentation at this stage often promotes the response in counsellors of 'more is better'. This is unhelpful. Brief interventions that allow the client time and space are much more effective.

Contemplation

At this stage the client is open to considering both the problem and change, yet remains undecided and ambivalent about taking action. Motivational enhancement therapy is particularly important at this stage: these skills are described in detail in the answer to Question 5.2. It is helpful to *empathize with and explore the client's ambivalence*, recognizing that contemplation is still not the same as commitment. *Information and education* that are personally relevant can promote the incentive to change. This can be undertaken in the context of self-monitoring questionnaires, drink/drug use diaries, blood tests and so on. *Decisional balance considerations* can be encouraged, looking at the pros and cons of the problem behaviour itself, and the pros and cons that making change is likely to promote. *Revisiting any past attempts at change* can be very productive in identifying those factors that were helpful, and those that were not so helpful.

Determination

Here the client is on the 'brink' of action. It is important for the counsellor to *assess the strength and level of commitment*. There is a difference between impassioned, but vague, statements of intent to change, and those that are based on a considered course of action. The counsellor can help the client in *assessing the difficulty* of the change plan, and look forward in a problem-solving way to any *anticipated difficulties* that may arise early on. The counsellor also needs to be sensitive to the client's determination as not unequivocal, and to *affirm ambivalence* as understandable.

Action

At this stage the clients are now implementing their own change processes. The counsellor's task is to remain present, continuing to *affirm and encourage the client's sense of personal responsibility and self-efficacy*. It is vital for the change to be internally, and not externally, attributed. It is important to be realistic: focus both on those areas where the client is doing well, so as to help perpetuate progress, and also on the more difficult areas, in order to *identify factors that may inhibit further action*; and then *work creatively in generating solutions*. This stage often requires practical responses from the counsellor, as action for the client may involve detoxification from drink or drugs, moving to a 'safer' environment such as an alcohol-free hostel and so on. Action from the client often demands action from the counsellor.

Maintenance

In this stage the new behaviour implemented in the action stage has become more robustly established. It is important that the counsellor still perceives this as an active, not passive stage and responds accordingly. The counsellor works with the client in consolidating changes made, particularly in the context of *relapse prevention* (see Questions 5.5. and 5.6). Equally the client might want to address those more personal intrapersonal and interpersonal difficulties that may have become apparent to the client once he or she has addressed the presenting problem. Within the field of substance misuse, there often appears a subtle, yet immensely significant, interplay between the client's substance use and the more personal factors that underlie it, which tends to emerge during this maintenance stage. Furthermore, if the client does not start to translate behavioural changes into more generalized, assimilated lifestyle changes, he or she can end up feeling trapped and powerless, often engendering a rather hopeless reaction of 'What now?' or 'What's the point?' Again, the counsellor needs to find the balance between *empathizing with the struggle* and *helping the client generate different ideas and options*.

Enhancing motivation and commitment through the stages

Miller and Rollnick (1991) identify eight strategies that are likely to enhance motivation and commitment in those contemplating change. However, provided the counsellor is sensitive to the client's stage of change and selects the intervention(s) accordingly, these strategies are useful at all stages, not least because of their practicality. Listed alphabetically for mnemonic purposes they are:

(a) Giving *Advice* – straightforward, non-judgemental advice that identifies the problem, explains the importance of change and offers an alternative.

(b) Removing *Barriers* – this is the pragmatic, straightforward consideration of providing accessible help, as well as assisting clients in addressing their own, practical, 'barriers' to change.

(c) Providing *Choices* – do not constrain clients with a single approach and facilitate their responsibility in making personal choices.

(d) Decreasing *Desirability* – work with clients on decreasing the perceived desirability of continuing with their current behaviour.

(e) Practising *Empathy* – this is not best described as a strategy, but better understood as a way of 'being with' clients.

(f) Providing *Feedback* – both practical in the form of information, suggestions, etc.; and in the sense of the counsellor being present and real.

(g) Clarifying *Goals* – help the client identify clearly what is to be changed and how.

(h) Active *Helping* – be active and affirmatively interested in the client's change process.

Paul Jackson

* * *

5.5 I have been told that relapse is a normal occurrence when working with this client group. If this is true, how can the counsellor help the client to avoid feeling a sense of failure?

Relapse is indeed a normal occurrence in many habitual behaviours. When it happens during the process of counselling, it can be a demoralizing experience for client and counsellor. Although it is hard to imagine not experiencing any sense of failure, it is possible to help clients cope with the feelings and also to view the relapse episode as a useful opportunity to gain new understanding. Preparing for the possibility of relapse needs to be done in a skilled and sensitive way, ensuring that it does not result in the client perceiving the counsellor as lacking faith in him or her. Helping clients cope includes providing an accepting, non-judgemental context to enable distressing thoughts and feelings to be addressed, and a way of understanding what may have precipitated the relapse.

Another element is to consider relapse as a process rather than an 'all-or-nothing' event, which often starts with a relatively harmless behaviour, more accurately described as a 'lapse'. This approach, drawing on a cognitive therapy model, involves explaining to clients a sequence of thinking patterns which commonly occur: having initially violated a self-imposed rule (such as 'I must not have even one sip of alcohol'), it is easy to use this as 'proof' that they are indeed helpless victims of some mysterious force and that they might as well carry on drinking. There is also an immediate reduction in self-esteem. The sense of being in control gives way to a sense of having no control and there is an attempt to reduce any contradiction between one's behaviour and one's self-image. Continuing to drink becomes a self-fulfilling prophecy. It appears that enabling clients to recognize and challenge such habitual ways of thinking can be a useful way of preventing relapse (Marlatt and Gordon 1985) and exploring these ideas in a counselling session after a relapse has occurred can be particularly powerful (see also Question 5.6).

'Post-relapse' counselling also means understanding the client's initial sense of things having gone horribly wrong and being able to empathize with this, whilst at the same time avoiding either colluding or catastrophizing. The core condition of acceptance provides reassurance for those who have been scarred by previous experiences of relapse. Friends and families are likely in the past to have expressed anger, disappointment, frustration, false reassurance, or may have inappropriately attempted to act as rescuer. Significant others frequently express criticism when people in therapy relapse, as they will have seen the individual begin to improve or cope and may be especially annoyed or disappointed at the notion that 'the treatment doesn't work'. A calm, impartial approach by the therapist will provide some counter-balance. The emphasis in the past may have been on the consequences for others of the client's behaviour. The counsellor will need to encourage the client to put himself or herself centre stage, rather than focusing on what effect the relapse had on other people or situations.

It is also crucial to address shame and guilt, a major component of which is often self-disgust at having failed to keep to a decision. The initial lapse into drinking or taking a drug may have brought immediate but temporary relief from feelings of vulnerability, confusion and distress.

As this effect wears off, other powerful negative thoughts and feelings will emerge, which are perceived as intolerable: they need to be fended off. Continuing with the lapse/relapse behaviour is likely to feel overwhelmingly familiar as the forces of self-loathing and desire for indulgence combine with a lack of self-efficacy, to produce a vicious circle that is hard to break. When a client has failed to prevent the initial lapse developing into a repetition of previously avoided behaviour, she or he may feel intense guilt because she or he has not used counselling properly, or because she or he feels she or he has let other people down. Her or his sense of loss of self-respect may increase as she/he indulges, but she/he may also need to indulge in order to cope with the feelings that well up.

Feelings of shame and guilt can be sufficiently strong that the client is unable to admit to having relapsed. Within a good therapeutic relationship, if a client hints about 'things going wrong', the counsellor should ask him or her to be concrete about how this has manifested itself. For example, the counsellor might say, 'It sounds as if the stress was becoming almost too much for you to bear. I guess swallowing a few tablets was a very tempting option? Is that what you did?' A balance can be struck between not enabling the client to continue to avoid the subject, and not appearing to assume that she or he had failed in some way.

Cultural norms, the setting in which counselling takes place and sub-cultural attitudes will play a significant part in how people feel and behave after a relapse. These will also affect what defences are erected to deal with the situation. Denial is, of course, a reaction to confrontation and may in the past for a client have been an automatic initial response to fend off fear, guilt, shame and loss of self-esteem. The norms of certain institutions, such as the probation service, are likely to engender various defensive postures that may make it difficult for honest and productive post-relapse counselling to take place. Other defensive strategies include minimizing, avoiding through 'not remembering' details, extreme dissociation ('It wasn't really me') or extreme passivity. The possibility of not being frank about setbacks should be acknowledged and discussed early in the development of the therapy – if necessary it should be addressed in the initial contract. Behind the defences, counsellors may find that the sense of failure which besets their clients is almost overwhelming.

What clients experience as 'relapse' can be worked on and understood as having at least some elements that make sense. In exploring these, it is likely that the counselling will need to emphasize the re-establishment of self-esteem, self-efficacy and improved coping responses. It will also be helpful to discuss the 'spiral' model of change with clients, indicating how insight and experiences gained as a result of a relapse episode will enable them to return either to re-evaluating choices about changing, or working on maintaining previously achieved gains.

I have emphasized the importance of the core conditions of empathy and acceptance in responding to relapse and the need to help clients use the experience as an opportunity to learn. Unfortunately, it is quite possible that the therapist's initial feelings on hearing that someone has relapsed could be anything from disappointment through to despair, puzzlement through to disbelief, mild irritation to downright anger. Pride in our work with clients and optimism about their future can be overturned in an instant. All these feelings are entirely understandable but they can certainly undermine counsellors' willingness and ability to work effectively with lapse and relapse.

Relapse can have a dramatic effect on therapy, leading either to a sudden moving forward, or to crisis, or to an impasse (Leiper and Kent 2001). The latter is likely if the counsellor fails to maintain neutrality, or ignores his or her own feelings and allows them to leak into the therapy sessions – for example, setting an inappropriately difficult homework task for a client, following discussion of a relapse, may be a way of punishing the client. The resulting resistance may lead to impasse and further feelings of frustration. Sometimes the counsellor expresses annoyance or disappointment directly – either verbally or nonverbally- and the client feels he or she is to blame and has no choice but to leave counselling.

Other feelings that may overwhelm the counsellor and get in the way are associated with taking up the position of 'rescuer' or 'victim'. These are the roles complementary to that of 'persecutor', described by Karpman (1968) who refers to the playing out of these interactions as the 'Drama Triangle'. Two, three or more people temporarily move into one of the three roles in response to a situation and to the role taken up by another significant person. If played out in a therapeutic situation, impasse or unplanned endings are inevitable. Thus the counsellor who feels great sympathy for the client who has relapsed may try to 'rescue' the client from a 'persecutory' world, colluding with or even pushing him or her into the role of 'victim'. Sometimes the counsellor may see the client as the persecutor and him- or herself as the victim.

Acknowledging and reflecting on feelings of failure associated with relapse contributes to normalizing the situation and moving forward. This may be done within supervision or outside of it – acknowledging disappointment or frustration in private with a colleague may be sufficient – prior to thinking about and then exploring how the client feels about it. Colleagues and supervisors need to beware of collusion (or rescuing or persecuting) and to be alert to the feelings in the counselling situation being replicated within supervision. There is no shame in feeling upset by a client's relapse: the therapist can in fact model for the client ways of dealing with it which are both honest and constructive.

Rose Kent

* * *

5.6 What can be done to minimize the tendency to relapse?

Relapse is a common phenomenon amongst people with addiction problems – before, during and following treatment. The last 20 years have seen an increasing interest in understanding and tackling relapse: this may partly be a reaction against practitioners in counselling and treatment settings focusing exclusively on getting clients to stop their alcohol or other drug use, but then being unsure how to help them maintain this. Clients are also often keen to focus on short-term goals – getting through the withdrawal symptoms – but may be reluctant to think about 'staying stopped'. The term 'relapse prevention' is now increasingly used to highlight this stage of treatment. Specific techniques based on cognitive behaviour therapy, with the emphasis on identifying triggers and modifying ways of thinking and reacting, have been popularized by Beck (1976), and Marlatt and Gordon (1985) and others. This approach can be satisfactorily incorporated into generic addictions counselling settings, and within Twelve Step treatment programmes, even though 'relapse' is given a slightly different emphasis in the latter approach.

Within the Twelve Step tradition and a medical model of treating alcohol and drug addiction, being on guard to prevent a 'slip' or relapse is seen as a permanent feature of having an addiction problem. Any return to the original behaviour, however brief or apparently insignificant, is seen as a slide down a slippery slope. Vigilance – the avoidance of picking up the drug or alcoholic drink in the first place – is seen as the fundamental skill required.

Although this section will use the terminology of 'relapse prevention' approaches, it is in fact more accurate to talk of minimizing, rather than preventing relapse, particularly within those models of addiction which emphasize the development of understanding and self-control in relation to the problem behaviour. From a social learning point of view, relapse is seen as a process, which can be interrupted and its harmful consequences reduced, if clients are trained to approach it in this way. Through analysing and understanding what factors contribute to the relapse, new and different behaviours can be learnt. The likelihood of relapse occurring therefore decreases over time and if it does occur, it will be less devastating for the individual and those around him or her.

Minimizing the tendency to relapse means that the counsellor needs adequately to prepare the client regarding how relapse will be handled within the counselling contract itself. It is essential to help clients recognize that relapse is not the end of counselling: indeed, very important therapeutic work can be done when clients are willing and able to discuss what went wrong. This means explaining in advance the counsellor's own likely responses. As discussed in Question 3.2, it is likely that in the past clients may have been reprimanded or rejected when they relapsed, which may contribute to their avoidance of working through relapse in subsequent treatment settings.

Having incorporated discussions about handling relapse during counselling in terms of the practical arrangements (such as the client arriving intoxicated) and the working alliance, the counsellor will need to make an assessment about the ways in which the client may be vulnerable to relapse. There are three levels of vulnerability: *enduring personal characteristics* and life circumstances, *high risk situations* relating to life events, and *lapses* (Leiper and Kent 2001).

Enduring personal characteristics

Some people with addiction problems have relatively stable characteristics that predispose them to relapse when temporary stressors occur. This first level of vulnerability may include personality variables such as chronic low self-esteem, social circumstances and chronic mental health difficulties (so-called 'dual diagnosis' clients). Counsellors need to acknowledge their own limitations in influencing this fundamental level of vulnerability. Clients may be lacking in social support, have poor physical health, be stigmatized and stereotyped, and efforts to provide long-term help are likely to be time-consuming. One could argue that, given the many different ways in which it is circumstance rather than individual predisposition that contributes the most to vulnerability to relapse, political and social change (rather than an individualistic approach) is the key factor in preventing relapse. Nonetheless, clients should be carefully assessed to identify those aspects that can be affected by psychotherapeutic interventions, in addition to forms of practical help being recommended – including the possibility of psychiatric or social interventions.

High risk situations

The second level – high risk situations identified with life events – includes less immediate and possibly cumulative triggers to relapse, and also those which may directly precipitate a relapse episode. Thus this level of vulnerability includes a range of events that most people would regard as stressful, such as redundancy, illness and relationship crises and also those specific situations which are unique to the individual – such as seeing an ex-partner unexpectedly with his/her new partner. It is at this level where cognitive-behavioural approaches are most relevant, involving the identification and monitoring of precipitating factors, the challenging of negative thoughts, coping and avoidance strategies, and the enhancement of self-efficacy through realistic goal setting.

Lapses

The third level of vulnerability to relapse is connected to the idea that returning to familiar but unwanted patterns of behaviour is not an event, but a process (Marlatt and Gordon 1985). The first step in the process is the violating of a self-imposed rule (for example, taking a sip of alcohol). The counsellor's intervention will involve assisting the client to identify the initial thoughts associated with this behaviour and enabling him or her to challenge notions of being 'out of control' at this point. This is a controversial view – many addictions therapists would argue that there is no turning back once this process has begun. Others believe that the inevitability of a 'lapse' becoming a full-blown relapse is a self-fulfilling prophecy, which can be challenged by learning about different ways of perceiving the situation.

Building awareness and gaining insight into when, where, how and why the temptation to revert to familiar patterns is greatest is for many people the single most helpful phase of recovery. Clients who are at the more severe end of the dependency continuum, or who have a very long history of addiction problems, may have become used to 'explaining' relapse as an irresistible response to a physiological craving. A social learning approach acknowledges the role played by physiological factors, including biochemical changes during the development of tolerance to a drug and the manifestation of physical discomfort during withdrawal, but emphasizes the learned associations between the drug-using environments, emotional states, and their accompanying physical manifestations. These physiological experiences will reduce over time, once the learned associations between drug taking and trigger situations are no longer reinforced.

Cognitive behaviour therapy is seen as one of the most effective approaches to minimizing the risk of relapse as it emphasizes first the monitoring of negative ways of thinking, and then the strategies for challenging and replacing them. Not every 'craving' leads to indulgence. Clients can normally identify when this element of personal control has occurred, and then build up a list of their unique ways of managing difficult situations. In addition new avoidance and coping strategies may need to be taught by the counsellor, including both new behaviours and 'self-talk'.

Clients may have tended towards extremely negative expectations of their own behaviour, and exaggerated positive effects of the drug – for example:

> If I don't get hold of a fix I'm going to go mad.

or

> There's no way I can possibly talk to my ex-girlfriend if I haven't had a few cans of lager.

Counsellors can help clients challenge and replace these habitual ways of thinking with realistic alternatives, such as:

> If I don't have a fix I'll feel uncomfortable for a while, but then the feeling will pass.

and

> It will be difficult talking to her completely sober, but I can walk away if I feel too bad.

Relapse prevention is likely to need to incorporate a range of behavioural and social skills: assertiveness, anger management, problem-solving skills, use of leisure time, re-entering employment, and mending family relationships. Relaxation and stress management, exercise and complementary therapies can also be useful.

Less experienced counsellors may underestimate just how 'naked' clients feel without their drug of choice to protect them from the world, and how long the period of adjustment to a new lifestyle may take. While client and counsellor may accept the inevitability of relapses during and possibly after a period of treatment, counselling or rehabilitation, and find ways of ensuring that he or she learns from them, other 'systems' of which the client is part may not see things this way. There may be people in the client's life who have attached an ultimatum to their help-seeking, along the lines of 'Stop drinking/using heroin completely this time or I will be putting the children on the child protection register/sending you to prison'. Setting aside the arguments for and against 'compulsory counselling', counsellors must address the fact that the client will probably experience extreme pressure from others in their environment *not* to relapse, while at the same time believing that they *will* relapse. It is important to clarify with clients the extent to which they want or expect you, the counsellor, to communicate with others involved in their treatment, and to be extremely sensitive to the possibility of unhelpful psychological games being played out. For example, the counsellor may be seen as the rescuer, the client as victim, and the other significant person (for example the probation officer) as persecutor. Similar dynamics can occur in relation to clients' families or partners, who can be very powerful in precipitating or preventing a relapse.

Clients may invest their counsellors with a lot of power, and covert anger, disappointment in, or idealization of, the counsellor can be a factor in contributing to relapse. By emphasizing homework tasks, having a clear and mutually agreed counselling contract, preparing ahead of time for periods of unavoidable absence and discussing the nature of the therapeutic alliance (the here-and-now of the counselling) at appropriate times, over-dependency on the counsellor can be kept in check. As the end of the counselling contract approaches, the client's feelings of anxiety or resentment should be recognized and addressed. A useful way of dealing with ending is to increase the period of time between counselling sessions gradually, for the last one-third of the counselling contract. It is also vital to make sure that clients understand that you as an individual, and the organizational setting in which you work, attaches no stigma to clients returning if/when a future relapse episode occurs and leads to particular difficulties or distress.

Rose Kent

* * *

5.7 Why do some people relapse less than others?

Many people who experience difficulties as a result of their substance use almost certainly respond by making changes with little or no assistance from others. Such individuals are not likely to be typical of those who approach the specialist facilities for help or for whom substance misuse seems to become a more entrenched difficulty. Many of the answers to questions in this book show what factors are likely to be associated with success in changing drug use, rather than with a tendency towards repeated relapse. Whilst it is possible to make some generalized statements about who may be more or less likely to relapse, it would be foolhardy to elevate any such guesses to the status of science.

Within the relapse prevention models, considerable emphasis is placed on the experience of control as being a powerful factor in determining the probabilities of future relapse episodes. More specifically, it is suggested that those who experience and enjoy adequate levels of self-control in relation to both drug use and other areas of their lives, are less likely to relapse than those who experience relatively lower levels of control. Many of those who have experienced difficulty with drug use in the past report having felt little or no agency as to what is happening to them. The contrasting experience of control, which may arise as a result of changing drug use, is not only very welcome, but also serves as a powerful reinforcer to maintain behavioural change.

Within the counselling relationship, it becomes very important that the client should feel a sense of 'ownership' for the process of change, as opposed to experiencing change as having been delivered by the counsellor. The aim is to provide a secure attachment that operates so as to empower the client rather than to nurture a dependency that disempowers. For many clients the experience of finding it possible to develop a helpful alliance with another person may comprise a very rare alternative to a past in which drugs have been regarded as offering a far more reliable means of response to personal need or of addressing life difficulties.

The capacity to experience and enjoy enhanced levels of self-control is highly contingent upon a number of variables, including the style of the therapeutic alliance, the experience that coping skills are available at times of difficulty, positive self-esteem, support from family and friends, the capacity to reflect accurately on one's circumstances, and of course the ability to enjoy security in matters such as housing, finance and relationships with others. For those who experience little sense of such control in their lives, drug use may continue to represent an attractive alternative, on the simple basis that it is something that the individual is able to 'do' in a situation in which other options seem very limited.

The importance of perceived self-control is relatively uncontroversial within the field of counselling. The majority of counsellors accept that they strive to enhance the autonomy and agency of their clients in general. However, it is important to acknowledge that some drug use may be important in its ability to assist the client in shedding controls – for example, by using alcohol to relax at the end of a hard day. Indeed, some clients may appear to 'break out' from aspects of their selves and/or their situations. The fact that drug use causes difficulty may in no way neutralize the persisting pleasurable effects experienced when certain control mechanisms are reduced through intoxication. With some clients, it is not unreasonable to suggest that drug use may even be connected to underlying masochistic tendencies in which the abandonment of self-control is sought.

The long-term drug-user who achieves change in drug use may be confronted with a situation in which the ability to enjoy increased levels of self-control may take some time to develop. Once again, this emphasizes the importance of the counsellor's ability to provide 'holding' for the client during the phase of transition. In the short term, a reduction in drug use may present the client with a very unpalatable situation, in which some of the pleasures/relief associated with drug use have been removed, and where difficulties that have been masked by previous drug use become more open to be experienced. The therapeutic alliance may function as a central means by which the client is able to successfully manage the hiatus occurring between the reduction of drug use, and the gradually increasing ability to enjoy the full benefits of such a change.

Bill Reading

CHAPTER 6

Controlling drug and alcohol use

6.1 People sometimes say 'once an addict, always an addict' – is this true?

As with many of the questions in this book, the answer to this is highly contingent upon the context in which it is being asked. The disease models of addiction tend to assert that those who develop problems with drug use are intrinsically different to those who do not do so. Within Alcoholics Anonymous, there is an aphorism that states: 'Alcoholism comes in people, not in bottles!' Those who have been more severely addicted to a drug are probably less likely to use that drug in anything other than an addictive pattern in the future (see Question 6.5). However, there are clearly many exceptions to this rule, and it is difficult to consider these matters properly without exploring the semantics of the question itself.

In the answers to some other questions (e.g. Question 5.2), the prominence of motivational enhancement therapy has been noted, and more particularly the contribution of social learning theory to this model: the quality of the interactions that an individual enjoys with others is a determinant of perception and behaviour. This emphasis provides a means of exploring this question from the point of view of the relationship between counsellor and client. More specifically, we can explore the quality of the interaction within the therapeutic alliance, which may influence the client's future perceptions and behaviours.

It is useful to employ a sociological model as a means of understanding the way in which 'labelling' can have profound implications for the client's sense of identity. Lemert (1966) suggests the important distinction between *primary deviance* and *secondary deviance* when considering the development of criminal identity. Lemert suggests that the committing of crime can be regarded as a form of primary deviance, in that it manifests a deviation from social norms and rules; whereas the penalties and responses of others to the person committing the crime might take the form of secondary deviance: for example, the labelling of an individual as 'criminal', with all the predictable consequences that are likely to ensue from such labelling, including those for the individual's inner sense of identity. The lawbreaker who becomes labelled as a criminal might be more likely to commit crimes in an attempt to deal with stigmatization and prejudicial responses from others. Hence a process of *deviance amplification* is initiated, with the social response increasing, rather than reducing, the possibility of further criminality.

If we transfer this model to consideration of drug use, it is easy to see ways in which individuals who use more drugs than others may be regarded as expressing a primary deviance; and how the responses of others may give rise to a series of interactions that result in secondary deviance.

The use of the term 'addict' may similarly give rise to a series of interactional processes that prepare the way for a particular form of deviance amplification, in which the individual becomes not only confirmed in the role of 'addict', but may also as a consequence become more likely to use drugs more excessively in the future: this arises in an attempt to adapt to the intrapersonal and interpersonal changes that have occurred as a result of such labelling.

Clients may have themselves established a tendency to mediate their perceptions of experience in ways that give prominence to substance-related phenomena. At the level of personal identity, the client may refer to experiences related to drug use in order to achieve a sense of self-definition, e.g. 'addict' or 'junkie'. Counselling can be of great importance in avoiding collusion with this view of the self and fostering the basis for other, less restrictive views. Equally, many clients seem to articulate personal experience in terms of drug use, rather than express emotional states and other aspects of themselves. The counsellor may therefore be able to assist the client to get in touch with feeling states that have become encoded within references to drug-taking. For example, the client's assertion that a particular difficulty led to strong cravings for drug use may be understood differently – 'I imagine that you may have been feeling very hurt, under the surface . . .'

While it is obvious that sensitive counsellors are unlikely to actually use the term 'addict' in conversations with clients, other more subtle communication may take place that nevertheless induces a degree of deviance/

addiction amplification. In keeping with the principles of motivational interviewing, every effort should be made to avoid the use of labels such as 'addiction' or 'dependency'; instead counsellors and therapists should attempt to keep in focus that the client is someone who happens to use drugs, rather than someone who is defined by their drug use. It may therefore be helpful for the counsellor to ask the following question: 'What view of the client is implied by the way I am relating to him or her?'

Bill Reading

* * *

6.2 What about 'cross-addiction'? Are people likely to have a tendency to get addicted to many things?

In thinking about this question, it is important to avoid the twin pitfalls of over-generalization on the one hand or gullibility on the other. An individual view of the situation is essential.

'Cross-addiction' can refer either to the presence of more than one addiction in the same individual, or to the assumed propensity of someone with an addictive problem to acquire or to replace one addiction by another. Some people, including some clients, refer to a kind of 'addictive personality' and tendency to excess. The expression 'poly-drug abuse' is also used, referring to the co-existence of different drugs of abuse in a given individual. Some argue that this is becoming more of a norm than in previous decades. Clearly, in taking a history of a person's addiction, it is important to consider the use of different drugs, perhaps during different periods of the individual's drug-taking career.

Many people with substance use disorders do present with a *single* 'drug of choice', such as heroin or alcohol. Although they may have experimented with other substances as part of the *history* of their problem, the current addiction is centred exclusively around this main drug. During the process of recovery, or of relapse after a period of abstinence, it is this particular drug that remains the key problem or preoccupation of the individual concerned. However, it is important to explore the possibility of poly-drug use, which may or may not be apparent at first glance (see Carroll 1986). Some of the more common examples of this are a heroin user who is also abusing alcohol on a regular or continual basis. Heroin users may also use cocaine or other stimulants, and often one form of drug is used to augment or to counteract the effect of another – such as the use of heroin to 'come down' following crack use. An alcohol client might also be using benzodiazepines, or possible other 'over the counter' legal drugs alongside the use of alcohol. Drugs like diazepam and temazepam may or may not have been prescribed, so it is important to consider legal as well as illegal drugs.

As to the process of recovery, some argue that people who have had an addiction remain vulnerable to substitution, and that it is hard to give something up without replacing it. The Fellowship organizations like AA and NA are cognizant of such risks in their thinking of addiction as a disease or as 'self-will run riot'. They constantly emphasize and remind the recovering individual of the risks of 'drug thinking', the desire to 'get high', or the wish to change the way they feel. It is well known that opiate users who have given up have a heightened risk of developing alcohol problems. Alternatively an alcoholic who is now dry may throw him- or herself into workaholic excess as a way of feeling good, or may get involved in dysfunctional relationships as a way of trying to solve basic problems of living. Clearly, from the point of view of the possible substitution of addictions, addiction *without* a drug is an important issue, be it relationships, work, gambling and so on (see Orford 2001).

It is helpful to conceptualize this problem in terms of a 'heightened risk' for the individual concerned. This notion avoids over-generalization, i.e. the suggestion that cross-addiction is inevitable, but points to a need for vigilance, both for the user and also the counsellor. The possible mechanisms involved in such vulnerability are unclear at this stage of our understanding, but there may be neuropsychological processes (involving particular brain functions), social factors (e.g. the influence of a particular peer group or milieu), or psychological deficits (whereby the individual seeks to 'fill' a hole by a similar solution).

Martin Weegmann

* * *

6.3 Is it necessary for a person to give up drugs or drinking completely if he or she has become addicted?

This question invites an extremely divergent set of answers, ranging from those who argue that only complete and lifelong abstinence from drugs will prevent the experience of further difficulty through to those who sometimes argue that being addicted to drugs represents as valid a form of existence as any other. For current purposes, this answer provides a functional framework in which to think about the implications of the question.

It has been suggested elsewhere in this book that all drug use carries with it some degree of risk. Those drugs that are more likely to result in the development of physical withdrawal symptoms carry with them the risk that their use will give rise to such symptoms. Accordingly, there is a logic that states that the only way to eliminate the risk of harmful consequences from drug use is to avoid using drugs at all. Approaches compatible with a strict abstinence from the use of intoxicants (or other supposed 'addictive behaviours') have proved successful to many millions of people worldwide. However, for many individuals the question whether to continue to use drugs, or to seek complete abstinence, becomes far more complex.

If one is inclined to view problematic drug use as demonstrating an inability on the client's part to exercise control or meaningful choice, one may also be inclined to regard the client's sentiments with regard to future drug use with some degree of suspicion. On the other hand, the view that drug-taking represents a chosen behaviour (albeit risky, but in common with other pursuits such as playing football or driving cars) is more likely to incline one to a position where the client's choices in these matters should be respected. Clearly one person's use of drugs may have implications for others. The 'right to take drugs' may need to be balanced against the right of others to be free from the consequences of an individual's drug use.

In the answer to Question 3.3, some factors were considered that might make it difficult for a client to acknowledge the difficulties that drug use has caused, and that may arise in the future. In situations in which it seems reasonable to suppose that the client is sufficiently aware of the *actual* likely consequences of further drug use, the counsellor may be quite prepared to both support the client's decision to continue using drugs *and* to help him or her avoid further problems wherever possible. Even in situations where the counsellor may feel that drug use is very likely to cause further difficulty, there may be more to gain from the counsellor's ability to adopt a 'wait and see' disposition, rather than the posture of a 'prophet of doom'. (Further consideration of the factors that may influence the success or otherwise of continued drug use are considered in Question 6.5. In answering Question 5.5, some of the issues are considered that are involved in continuing to work with clients who continue to use drugs.)

Bill Reading

* * *

6.4 What if the counsellor believes that a client is being unrealistic in trying to reduce drug use rather than stopping it altogether?

It is difficult to answer this question without first noting the crucial significance of the quality of the therapeutic alliance in determining how such a situation might be addressed. The client who experiences the counsellor as genuinely committed to promoting what seems best for the client's interests will respond quite differently to the client who experiences the counsellor as an adversary, whose ministrations must be treated with suspicion. Some clients present in contexts in which an 'adversarial' quality becomes more likely – for example, those experiencing excessive coercion to engage in counselling. Others may be sensitive to the threat to the relationship to the drug of choice, which is perceived as accompanying the counsellor's attempts to provide help (Reading 2001). Where clients experience profound levels of ambivalence about drug use, it is not surprising that transference/counter-transference configurations are evoked, within which the counsellor may be experienced as opposing the client's relationship with drugs – perhaps an example of a 'invalidating fantasy' enactment referred to in the answer to Question 3.7. With such a scenario, it is possible that the client engages in an (externalized) dialogue, in which the aim is to both solicit and repel the counsellor's attempts to persuade the client to 'stop using drugs'. The potential usefulness of the client's capacity for 'internal ambivalence' is clearly reduced in such a setting.

Where sufficient trust exists within the alliance, the counsellor is better able to express concern about the client's plans for future drug use, as well as the basis upon which such concern is founded. In keeping with the principles of motivational enhancement therapy discussed elsewhere (e.g. Question 5.2), the counsellor attempts to *'roll with* the resistance', rather than engage in argument with the client. I have experienced numerous occasions where clients report how they have been able to defy the negative predictions of 'helpers' whose predictions did not materialize. As counsellors, we may legitimately offer our best advice based on evidence, concern for the client's welfare and discussion of potential risk. But categoric assumptions as to what will happen in a client's life as a result of further drug use are an invitation to the counsellor to adopt the role of omnipotent and omniscient authority figure rather than that of the dedicated helper.

However, there may be circumstances in which the potential risks of a client's continued drug use are so extreme or otherwise unacceptable to the counsellor that the counsellor feels that collaboration with the client at such points is unacceptable and dangerously collusive. For example, the counsellor may feel unable to cooperate with a client who expresses a wish to continue to use alcohol, despite a known history of severe medical damage as a result of previous drinking, such as cirrhosis of the liver. Alternatively, continued drug use may be regarded as representing an unacceptable risk of severe harm to others, such as those inclined to perpetrate violence or sexual abuse when intoxicated. In extreme situations the counsellor may regard it as unethical to continue to work with a client under such circumstances, and may need to consider other options, such as taking advice from his/her ethics panel, specialist supervision or onward referral. Inevitably, should any of these measures be considered, sensitive consideration needs to be given to the client's feelings about being rejected, their ability to attach to another helper, and so on. One dilemma is that to cease working with the client may exacerbate the very risks that have given cause for concern in the first place, for example, where a client may resort to using drugs even more heavily in response to the counsellor's decision to discontinue the relationship. It is at times such as this that the support of colleagues and others can prove invaluable, as the counsellor attempts to grapple with the best way in which to resolve such dilemmas.

Bill Reading

* * *

6.5 Is it possible to predict whether a client has a good chance of reducing drug use without stopping it altogether?

Although it may seem rather obvious, the most potent predictor of whether or not a client will be able to reduce drug use is probably to be found in the degree of commitment that a client has towards maintaining a reduced level of usage in the future. Such commitment is expressed through what it is that the client *wants* to do about his or her drug use. This is not to suggest simply that the client who wishes to reduce drug use will be successful, but to acknowledge that a reduction in drug use is only likely to occur where this has been the genuine wish of the client. As discussed in the answer to Question 6.4, it is helpful to establish how realistic the client's perceptions are, in terms of previous experience and other variables that are likely to influence the outcome, i.e. whether or not reduced use is maintained in the future. What follows are some suggestions as to those factors that might be considered in trying to help the client establish a pattern of reduced drug use rather than stopping the use of drugs completely. This assumes that the client is in a position to *choose* which goal(s) to pursue. There are different considerations where changes in behaviour are imposed by others.

Level of physical addiction

With regard to drugs recognized as producing physiological withdrawal states, such as heroin, alcohol, crack cocaine and others, it is generally safe to assume that the more severe the level of physical addiction (as gauged by severity and chronicity of withdrawal symptoms), the more difficult it will be to maintain a reduction to lower levels of consumption in the future. In some situations, even after the individual has not used the drug for an extended period of time it seems as if there is a persisting 'addiction memory' (Edwards 2000); the individual finds that he or she reverts to very high levels of consumption, sometimes rapidly, once drug use has resumed. In some instances, it is possible to explain this effect as a result of neuro-adaptation and other physiological changes, which lead the individual to acquire a persisting high tolerance to particular drugs, and an exaggerated propensity to experience withdrawal symptoms, particularly at high levels of consumption. Clients who have found that they regularly 'reinstate' former elevated levels of consumption, tolerance and withdrawal effects in the past may have less favourable prospects of maintaining reduction in the longer term than those who have been able to maintain reduced levels of consumption in the past. Although the degree of past physical addiction functions as an important guide as to what is possible, there are many individuals who have been able to revert to lower levels of consumption, despite having had a significant history of physical addiction in the past.

Chronicity of heavy drug use

The drug-user who has experienced a recent, short-lived and uncharacteristic increase in drug use related to particular circumstances may have a relatively good change of reducing drug use in the future. On the other hand, the client who has been using drugs heavily for many years with few or no periods of controlled use, relatively regardless of external circumstances and life events, may be in a much less favourable position. Clearly, the extent of a client's drug use may be closely related to age, with younger clients tending to have less enduring histories of drug use than their older counterparts. Many individuals seem (spontaneously) to use drugs less frequently and heavily as they increase in age (see Question 2.5). It is sometimes suggested that the capacity for flexibility and adaptability may decrease with advancing age, with the effect that the 'less adaptable' client may have greater difficulty in changing old habits. However, it is not uncommon to see relatively young individuals whose drug use is of such an intensity and degree that any reduction in consumption is difficult to imagine.

Level of social stability

Individuals with reasonable levels of social stability (i.e. satisfactory accommodation, secure relationships, gainful employment/occupation and so on) may be better placed to reduce drug use than those who have more chaotic lifestyles. Of particular importance is the degree to which individuals have social networks that could support and reinforce a reduction in consumption, as distinct from those whose social affiliations are exclusively with others who would be unsupportive in this respect.

Belief system

The client who believes that any degree of drug use activates a disease process, which compels the person to 'lose control' of consumption, is much less likely to sustain a reduction in consumption than the client whose belief system suggests that such a reduction ought to be feasible.

Therapeutic ambience

The client who wishes to reduce consumption of drugs will fare better if engaged in a therapeutic environment (including that with the individual counsellor) in which support for such a strategy is available. It is not suggested that the counsellor should engage in any form of 'pseudo-reassurance', or other forms of unfounded optimism. Rather, the counsellor should be open to assist the client in genuine attempts to effect a reduction, and able to continue to remain alongside the client, regardless of whether the current strategy seems to be succeeding or failing. The counsellor's ability to express a genuine 'therapeutic commitment' is more likely to assist the client achieve his or her goals, whatever they may be.

Modes of harm

The preceding factors are largely the degree of probability that future reduced consumption is possible. This last factor has regard for the form and severity of harm that the person has experienced as a result of previous drug use. There may be situations in which the client might otherwise be thought to have a good chance of reducing drug use, yet where there is reason to suppose that even considerably reduced levels may give rise to unacceptable levels of harm. For example, the client who has repeatedly experienced epileptic-type fits upon withdrawal of alcohol may be at considerable risk of experiencing such fits again, even at much reduced levels of consumption. Some clients may undergo severe feelings of paranoia after relatively low levels of consumption of stimulants, such as amphetamine or cocaine.

A consideration of the potential consequences of future consumption of drugs, even at reduced levels, should play an important part in attempts to help the client decide whether attempts at reduced consumption are wise. In considering this dimension, it is helpful to think in terms of the potential vulnerability to experiencing harm that appears to be characteristic of the client, and that may exist relatively independently of the level of consumption. For example, in the examples cited above, the disposition to experience fits after consumption of alcohol, and the vulnerability towards feelings of paranoia when using stimulants, might be matters that require careful consideration in the client's attempt to find the best future strategy.

Bill Reading

* * *

6.6 I've heard of 'controlled drinking'. Is this the same as 'social drinking'?

The terms 'controlled drinking' and 'social drinking' may be used in poorly defined ways and sometimes interchangeably. The 'social drinking' of a rugby team celebrating its latest victory is likely to be very different from that taking place where alcohol forms a part of a religious ritual. However, it is possible to draw a distinction here that can be used when helping clients to attempt to make changes in their use of alcohol.

Although the term 'social drinking' has various connotations, it is probable that most social drinking is appropriate to the particular social context in which it occurs. Moreover, the extent of consumption will also reflect the prevailing context. The limit that the social drinker applies to his or her consumption is likely to be the result of quite spontaneous, intuitive decision-making, often consonant with the limits that others are setting in the same situation. Some social drinking may appear to be quite controlled, whereas clearly excessive levels of consumption may still be regarded as 'social' in particular situations.

The term 'controlled drinking' tends to be used of situations where individuals are attempting to use alcohol in ways that differ from previous episodes of consumption, most notably in attempting to drink less heavily. Many who have consumed alcohol excessively in the past have discovered that their spontaneous ability to gauge or manage consumption has proved to be unreliable. Essentially, controlled drinking requires the individual to apply a series of conditions and limits upon alcohol use, with a view to avoiding further episodes of excessive or problematic drinking (Heather and Robertson 1983). In contrast to the social drinker, the controlled drinker is much more likely to be making a series of systematically derived cognitive decisions about consumption in any given situation. Question 6.7 considers some of the measures that may be helpful when clients are trying to implement controlled drinking or drug use.

Bill Reading

* * *

6.7 What rules should a person adopt in order to keep in control of his or her drinking or drug use?

The primary consideration here is that raised by the issues in Question 6.5. The client who wishes to continue to use drugs, and who believes that reduced use ought to be possible, can be helped to identify a series of conditions which if applied to future drug use will reduce or eliminate the potential to experience further episodes of harm and/or excessive consumption. Many drug and alcohol agencies are able to supply useful literature regarding controlled and reduced drug use. Miller and Munoz (1982) provide a comprehensive account of measures and procedures of use in managing alcohol use.

A helpful starting place is to help the client identify what he or she hopes will be the desirable outcomes of continuing to take the drug in question, and also what consequences the client wishes to avoid in the future. The measures that might comprise a 'controlled drug use programme' should be those that are compatible with delivering these desired effects together with avoiding the unwanted effects of drug use. The measures that a particular client needs to apply to avoid harm vary, but the following factors are probably those that need to be considered when helping most clients to establish conditions of use that will produce the desired outcome.

Pattern of consumption

Consideration should be given to the *quantity*, *quality* and *frequency* of consumption (see Question 4.7). It is generally not difficult to establish the point above which consumption is likely to give rise to problems and, conversely, below which drug use ought to be relatively safe. Attention to the quantity, quality and frequency of drug use starts to expose the ways in which the pattern of consumption might be manipulated in order to reduce the propensity to experience harm. The degree of intoxication achieved during a drug-taking session may be a crucial factor in determining whether or not the client continues to remain in a position of control. Controlled drinking or drug use requires the client to persist in implementing pre-determined decisions about the nature of consumption, and to monitor the current situation accurately. Clearly, both of these latter functions may be compromised by increasing levels of intoxication, because the client's very perceptual apparatus becomes affected as intoxication increases. A powerful example exists in the instance of alcohol-related road traffic accidents where intoxication through alcohol can give rise to a potentially deadly cocktail – an enhanced sense of one's ability to negotiate a risky situation, combined with objective reductions in actual performance.

Mood state

Many clients report that levels of drug consumption are closely linked to particular mood states, with some states consistently associated with much higher levels of consumption than others. For example, those who begin using drugs when feeling particularly distressed may not only require stronger drug effects but also be relatively unconcerned as to the possibility for negative consequences. Conversely, consumption of drugs in relation to other mood states may have been consistently safe in the past. Within the fellowship of Alcoholics Anonymous, it is not uncommon to hear reference to the 'H.A.L.T. Principle' whereby members are encouraged to be particularly careful to avoid becoming 'Hungry, Angry, Lonely or Tired'. Some women report significantly different responses to the use of drugs at varying points in the menstrual cycle.

The role of other drugs

Where the client uses several drugs simultaneously, it is important to consider the effect that various combinations may have upon the ability to retain a sense of *cognitive vigilance*. For example, the use of amphetamine dramatically increases tolerance to alcohol, so that the individual may consume much larger amounts than otherwise. Conversely, the consumption of benzodiazepines (e.g. valium, mogadon) greatly potentiates the effects of alcohol.

Choosing the right context

Some situations are far more conducive to heavy consumption than others. Included in these are those that involve the people with whom the client might be taking drugs. It may be helpful to identify relatively safe situations and people, and to avoid consumption in contexts which are relatively less safe.

Identification of early warning signals

The client can be helped to identify potential circumstances or consequences of consumption which provide a warning signal that it is necessary for him or her to take avoiding or preventative action. Cues that might alert each client are highly variable, but can be usefully established through analysis of past situations in which there may have been difficulty.

Maintaining cognitive vigilance

Particularly in the early stages of an attempt to control drug use, it can be helpful to build in measures to help the client resist the tendency to revert to more complacent or casual attitudes to consumption. Talking regularly with the counsellor can be important in this respect. This monitoring function can be supplemented through the use of written records of drug use, with a particular view to seeing whether the client is managing to keep within the controls and measures that had been thought to be helpful. Additionally, the use of some form of 'drug-taking diary' can be helpful in the process of helping the client to identify those aspects of current consumption that provide opportunities for change.

Ideally, controlled drug use and/or drinking is of the kind that confers only positive benefits upon the individual with few or no adverse consequences. It is perhaps important to bear in mind that many clients have a long history of having used drugs and of regarding some degree of harm as an acceptable price to pay. The client may wish to use drugs in a way that reduces but does not completely eliminate the potential harm. Perhaps one of the most important functions of the counsellor in this situation is to enable the client to form an honest judgement about the actual costs and benefits of continued drug use, and to avoid the pitfalls arising from attempts to adapt to a fantasized rather than the actual situation.

Bill Reading

* * *

6.8 How can one tell if a client is managing to control his or her drug use?

In answering this question let us assume a scenario where the client has identified a substance misuse problem and has made healthy, observable changes to this during the course of counselling.

Are clients who misuse substances honest?

This is an important consideration in answering this question, since perceptions of the client's 'character' can greatly influence the process of *how* the counsellor establishes whether his or her drink/drug use is being managed. Since the counsellor is reliant upon the client's 'self-reporting' to a great extent, a robust therapeutic alliance becomes central.

There appears to be no evidence to suggest that those who misuse substances are any more or less honest than those that do not. However, there still persists a belief in many quarters that they are, and in part this can be understood historically as relating to moral and medical models of addiction that have attributed all kinds of undesirable personality traits and deficits. Question 3.11 addresses this issue more fully. However, it also needs to be acknowledged that, for anyone, external and internal factors sometimes influence the client's ability or wish to be honest. For example, a client living in 'alcohol-free' accommodation, where his residence is contingent upon his abstinence, has a drink. If no one else knows, does he tell his counsellor? An internal factor is seen in the client who has been drug-free for sometime, and has evolved a whole new sense of himself based on this abstinence. Any lapse may be experienced as intolerable to this self-image. One way of resolving this conflict, albeit an uneasy one, is simply to 'forget' that it happened. Ways of increasing the possibility of an open relationship are discussed below. However, the counsellor always needs to have as a starting point the belief that the client will act in good faith. This is not to advocate naiveté: but it is better to be optimistic about the integrity of clients and risk being disappointed on occasion, rather than being cynical and having to be proved right.

The therapeutic relationship

The best way of establishing whether the client is controlling his or her drink/drug use is simply for the client to tell the counsellor what is happening, and for the counsellor to feel free to ask. In reality of course other factors will impinge upon this, as indicated above; but 'openness' will be fostered by the counsellor's attendance to those factors that promote a healthy therapeutic relationship.

The counselling contract

Usually in counselling and therapy, contracting with clients attends to more structural factors such as frequency of sessions, issues of confidentiality, identifying specific difficulties to be worked on and so forth.

In working with substance misuse difficulties, the counsellor needs to be very specific in agreeing definable, observable criteria that can objectively measure change. It is difficult to tell if a client is managing his or her drink/drug use if it has not been established clearly what 'managing' means. What 'managing' means is self-defining if the client is wishing to maintain abstinence; but things are not so clear-cut if the client is aiming for controlled or attenuated drinking/drug use. Furthermore, many clients want to address only one aspect of their drink/drug use, and continue with other substances; or they may be on prescribed 'maintenance' medication such as methadone (see Question 6.9), or on psychotropic drugs like tranquillizers and antidepressants. In these cases, it can be difficult to establish what effects are being caused by the presence of certain drugs, what is related to the combination of certain drugs, and what results from the absence of certain drugs.

Defining 'managing' in these circumstances can be very complex. Such negotiations require the counsellor to be quite active, as the client often needs help in articulating the meaning of statements such as 'I want to cut down a bit', and then in forming this into something concrete that can be worked with. This also needs sensitivity from the counsellor, since moving from a generalized statement to specifics can be a daunting process for the client. Making these criteria part of the formal treatment contract normalizes reference to it, and this in turn means there is a shared, counsellor/client agreement that managing will be a consistent point of discussion.

An important part of these negotiations is to encourage realism: these are agreed goals and criteria to be aimed for, but if they are not achieved or maintained the client still attends and will still be well received by the counsellor. Establishing early on that the counselling alliance is based on working together towards a shared aim and not just when the client seems to be doing well is one way of facilitating an open, honest relationship. Another factor that helps in maintaining a shared focus is to build in agreed times for review and appraisal, and these are obviously contingent upon the client and counsellor first defining what is to be reviewed or appraised.

Establishing measurable criteria

These criteria can be many and varied, but must always be negotiated. Some of them will be very practical, others more 'interactive'. Each therapist has to consider their applicability in the context of his or her own philosophy and practice.

Blood/saliva testing and urine screening

These can be 'scientific' measures of change: a baseline for establishing the presence of drugs/alcohol in the body. As an example, a client drinking heavily may demonstrate altered liver function tests due to his or her alcohol use. One goal of treatment that has a measurable outcome may be to repeat these tests at regular intervals as the client reduces drinking or establishes a period of abstinence. In the normal manner of things, the client's liver function tests will gradually move back towards the normal range over a period of time. A criterion like this often has a very motivating effect on the client, not least because he or she can objectively see the harm that drinking has caused and the benefits that reduction promotes. Equally, if the client's liver function tests reduce and then start to raise again, suggesting further drinking, this cannot be ignored, since the 'objective data' bring this possibility into the counselling relationship as something to address.

Questionnaires and rating scales

There are many monitoring aids that can be used in the area of substance misuse that are applicable through the whole course of change. Some are used on assessment only; others are used throughout for comparison; and others focus on certain events such as relapse or factors that may precipitate this. Equally, other measures may be used that are not specific to addictions, but relate to more general experiences such as depression or anxiety. As these difficulties are often caused or exacerbated by drink and drug use, measuring these in a comparative sense can also help establish to what extent the client is managing to control his or her substance use. For example, drink-related anxiety will reduce with abstinence.

Self-monitoring and reporting

Most often this is in the form of drink/drug use diaries, in which the client records his or her daily use over a period of time. Usually these diaries are set out in a way so that the client not only records actual consumption over a day, but describes and relates this both to situational factors and to personal feeling states. In this way, the client ends up with a 'snapshot' not only of amounts, but also of situational and personal factors that relate to the process of his or her substance use. Furthermore, with diaries it is easy to compare actual consumption with that which was agreed.

Secondary outcome measures of change

Sometimes clients like to define an outcome that is not a direct measure of their substance use but is one which they feel is only achievable or sustainable if changes to substance use are made and maintained. For example, a client keeps a job which was under threat due to his drinking; or another client returns to play a sport which she had ignored when heavily using drugs.

Observable measures

These are not scientific or objective, but relate to 'knowing the client':

1. Most obviously, the physical presentation of the client: the client who has successfully negotiated a period of reduced drink/drug use looks different from the way he or she was initially, when using drink or drugs heavily.
2. Attending in a state of withdrawal, or obviously under the influence of drugs or alcohol: this is still applicable even if the client is not required to be substance-free for the sessions, since a contract is likely to include defined parameters beyond which the client might be deemed too intoxicated to reasonably use the sessions.
3. Re-emergence of factors previously associated with the client's substance use: for example, suicide attempts, cutting and other acts of self-harm, 'unexplained' injuries and so on.

If the client does not relate these factors to the possibility of increasing substance misuse, then the counsellor needs to do so, sensitively but firmly. The counsellor will feel more able to do this where a clear and definable counselling contract was initially established.

Intuitive measures

Once again, these very much relate to 'knowing the client'. In the relationship the counsellor often gets an intuitive sense of 'things not being quite right', even if overtly the client seems fine:

1. The client seems to be talking from a different position about his or her drink/drug use, such as producing reasons why using again, or using heavily, would not be such a bad idea.
2. The client diminishes or trivializes the experience of reducing his or her substance use.
3. The client misses or cancels sessions when he or she had previously been a consistent attender.
4. The client is vague or elusive when his or her substance use is discussed.

If the counsellor has this intuitive sense, then it is of course the counsellor's responsibility to decide how to respond. In the context of a solid therapeutic relationship, it is likely to be facilitative to 'wonder' sensitively with the client about the apparent discrepancy between what is being said and what the counsellor is experiencing.

Finally, it needs to be acknowledged that establishing whether or not clients are managing their substance use can at times prompt interactions that promote intense feelings within the relationship, for client and counsellor alike. The counsellor needs to somehow strike a balance: being consistent and focused while not becoming intrusive or persecutory.

Paul Jackson

* * *

6.9 Can prescribed drugs help to reduce a client's reliance on drink or drugs?

Drugs are sometimes prescribed to reduce a person's dependence on drink or drugs. Such prescribing should not take place except as part of a package of treatment, which includes psychological treatment and support. The aims of prescribing, and the duration and criteria by which progress will be assessed, should be clearly set out and agreed beforehand.

In opiate addiction, *methadone*, a long acting opiate, is often prescribed either for detoxification from other opiates or for maintenance treatment. Even if detoxification is the eventual aim a period of stabilization, in which no reduction in the methadone dose is made, may last for weeks or months before detoxification commences.

Prescribing methadone does not of course reduce the client's dependence on opiates. It is the substitution of addiction to one opiate, such as heroin, by dependence on methadone, another opiate. However, the consumption of methadone has considerable advantages over the consumption of other opiates. Because it is taken orally, there are none of the risks associated with injection. Methadone has a long half-life and only needs to be taken once daily. Because its level in the bloodstream falls slowly, it is less likely to give severe withdrawal symptoms than other opiates. Prescribed methadone is of pharmacological purity and has reliable and predictable effects, unlike illegal sources of supply, where concentrations of the active drug vary considerably, often being mixed with other substances.

Once people are stabilized on methadone, they no longer have to engage in crime or prostitution to obtain funds for drugs; they do not have to spend large amounts of time in obtaining drugs; and they are not continually suffering the alternating effects of drug intoxication and withdrawal. This should enable them to engage in a more stable lifestyle, to find accommodation and occupation, and reduce criminal activity. It also allows them to engage in counselling or drug treatment, in which they can examine the role of drugs in their life, and consider whether they wish to withdraw from drugs altogether. There is now substantial evidence from clinical trials that for those patients who are able to engage in methadone maintenance as part of a structured programme of treatment, there is reduction in injecting behaviour, illicit drug use, criminal activity and other costs to society as a whole.

There are, however, some possible problems with such programmes. Methadone does not produce a 'high' or feeling of euphoria, and other drugs may be taken in addition in order to procure this effect. To prevent this, random urine tests for drugs are performed in most methadone programmes. Methadone may also be sold on, or exchanged for illegal drugs, so consumption of the daily dose may often occur under supervision. Although methadone protects drug-users from drug-related harm, it is not completely safe. In England and Wales, the number of drug-related deaths associated with methadone is consistently two to three times higher than the number of deaths associated with heroin. In 1994, there were 259 deaths involving methadone, and 90 deaths with heroin. In 1996, there were 357 and 187 deaths respectively. Many of these deaths occur as the result of drug overdose, especially where there are interactions with other drugs or with alcohol.

Patients taking methadone are continuously under the influence of a powerful mood-altering drug. There are specific ways of working psychologically with such patients, but many forms of counselling or psychotherapy depend on the client being fully alert and emotionally reactive. The general counsellor or psychotherapist may feel that it is inappropriate to engage with a client who is taking psychotropic drugs, although this depends on the therapist's background, experience and beliefs. If such a client is referred and the therapist feels uncomfortable about it, it is better to refer the patient on to specialist services, or to someone whose therapeutic approach is felt to be more appropriate.

Buprenorphine is another opiate that is occasionally used for opiate withdrawal or opiate maintenance treatment. The principles applying to its use are the same as those for methadone.

Methadone is rather exceptional in that equivalent 'substitute' drugs have not been developed for substances other than the opiates. While some drugs may act as a temporary 'substitute' during the phase of with-drawal, they are not suitable for more long-term use or maintenance. If such drugs are used in the longer term, they invariably give rise to prob-lems in their own right. For example, diazepam may be used to replace alcohol for one to two weeks, but is likely to give rise to tolerance and withdrawal symptoms if used beyond this.

Heminevrin (chlormethiazole) is another drug that is sometimes used to control alcohol withdrawal symptoms, but again is problematic if used in the longer term. Heminevrin is also particularly dangerous if taken simul-taneously with alcohol and should only be used in controlled, in-patient settings.

Bill Plummer

* * *

6.10   Are there prescribed drugs that can put people off using alcohol or drugs?

There are a number of drugs that help people who are abstinent from drugs or alcohol to avoid relapsing into substance misuse. Two main groups of drugs are helpful in this area: those that reduce or prevent crav-ings; and those that put people off from using substances, by nullifying the desired effects, or producing unpleasant side-effects.

Reducing/preventing cravings

In the first category two drugs have been introduced quite recently that seem to be effective for some people in preventing relapse when combined with ongoing psychological treatment and support. The first of these is *acamprosate* (Campral EC), said to work by reducing cravings for alcohol. The second is *bupropion* (Zyban), used in treatment for smoking cessation.

Acamprosate is commenced once abstinence from alcohol has been achieved, and may be continued if the patient has minor lapses into drinking. It should be discontinued if the patient has a major relapse into alcohol abuse. It should only be used in conjunction with ongoing psychological treatment and support. It seems to have a fairly specific effect in reducing cravings for alcohol, and does not have much mood-altering activity. In general its use is unlikely to prevent someone from engaging effectively in counselling or psychotherapy.

Bupropion is used in courses of up to nine weeks, in conjunction with psychological treatment, to help people reduce and stop cigarette smoking. Because smoking is such a serious public health issue, the use of this drug is quite strongly supported by the British government at present. The drug does have some dangers, however, as it lowers the threshold for epileptic fits, especially in combination with some drugs used for preventing malaria.

Putting people off substance use

Drugs that discourage relapse by producing unpleasant side-effects, or by nullifying the desired effects of the abused drug, include *disulfiram* and *naltrexone*.

Disulfiram (Antabuse) is used to prevent relapse in alcohol abuse. Once this drug is taken, if even a tiny amount of alcohol is consumed, it produces very unpleasant reactions, including flushing of the face, headache, palpitations, nausea and vomiting. This reaction can be dangerous – if larger doses of alcohol are taken, collapse and death may occur – and so this drug must be used with caution. The patient must avoid accidental ingestion of alcohol, small amounts of which are found in medicines. Even toiletries and mouthwashes may provoke a reaction. Disulfiram is taken daily, but the effects last for several days. In spite of the dangers of this drug, and the risk of unpleasant reactions, it is quite popular amongst people with drinking problems, many of whom find it helpful in preventing relapse. Essentially, the drug works by removing the need to make the decision not to drink in situations where force of habit or of circumstance are likely to cause relapse. Once someone has taken the tablet for the day, which itself becomes a matter of habit, they know that they cannot drink alcohol for several days, no matter how sorely they are tempted to do so.

Naltrexone is used in the treatment of opiate dependence, again to prevent relapse. It occupies the opiate receptors of the nerve cells and blocks the action of opiates, without itself having any opiate activity. It should only be used once a person has been abstinent from opiate drugs for seven to ten days. If it is given when someone is still under the influence of opiates, it could provoke a severe withdrawal reaction. Once it is being taken, any opiates consumed have no effect, so there is no incentive to relapse into using these drugs.

Bill Plummer

CHAPTER 7

Legal matters

7.1 Do I have a legal duty to inform the police if I discover that a client is using or dealing in drugs?

If a client tells you in the course of counselling or psychotherapy that he or she is using or dealing in drugs, then the normal principles of professional confidentiality apply. The client is entitled to expect you to keep a confidence, except where there are compelling reasons not to do so because of an over-riding public interest.

Usually in the course of a counselling relationship, the client only raises such issues because he or she is concerned about them. In many cases, the client wishes to change his or her behaviour and expects to be able to discuss personal worries and concerns without the fear of exposure to outside agencies.

The principle of confidentiality is enshrined in all professional codes of conduct, and is an essential element of professional relationships. Because there is a public interest in maintaining confidentiality it is also in many cases a legal requirement. For example, patient confidentiality is a requirement in most NHS staff contracts. Disclosure of confidential information can lead to legal action for breach of confidence. The European Convention on Human Rights and Fundamental Freedoms, a framework for legislation in the European Union, has recently been accepted by the United Kingdom. Article Eight states: 'Everyone has the right to respect for his private and family life, his home and correspondence.' This has been interpreted by the European Court of Human Rights as affording protection to individual privacy.

However, the right to confidentiality is not absolute. Sometimes there may be a legal or statutory requirement to break confidentiality. On other occasions the professional may decide to break confidentiality because of an over-riding public interest. Before doing so, it is wise to seek professional and legal advice. In relation to the present question, disclosure of a crime is not held to be in the public's interest unless it is 'iniquitous'. Possession or use of drugs, or minor drug dealing, may not be 'iniquitous', but serious crime such as major drug dealing could well be.

One way in which the law in the United Kingdom differs from that in the United States is that in the United Kingdom there is no requirement to disclose confidential information revealed by clients to third parties who may otherwise suffer harm. Following the Tarasoff case in the USA, practitioners who fail to reveal such information to third parties, who subsequently suffer harm, may be liable to claims of negligence. As a result, professionals in the USA are much more likely to breach confidences.

There are, of course, other accepted conditions in which confidentiality can be broken. For example, information can be passed on after seeking the client's consent, and information necessary for a patient's treatment can be passed between health professionals.

In the case of drug or alcohol abuse, there is one statutory requirement which applies only to doctors. Until 1997, doctors were required to notify the Home Office of all cases of addiction to certain drugs. Since that date, they are required to report all cases of drug misuse to the relevant Regional Drug Misuse Database. Reporting should take place when a patient first presents with a drug problem or re-presents after a gap of more than six months. These databases contain anonymous data which is used for epidemiological purposes.

The Police and Criminal Evidence Act 1984 provides for access to medical and other professional records by the police when undertaking an investigation, by applying for a warrant from a circuit judge. In general, medical or counselling records are not protected by any form of privilege, and must be disclosed when disclosure is requested during judicial proceedings.

If the professional is not told by the client that the client possesses or is dealing in drugs but discovers this by another means, then the rules of confidentiality do not apply. There is still not a legal requirement to pass this information on to the police, but the professional is not prevented from doing so. It is a matter of personal conscience. Of course, the counsellor may wish to discuss this with the client before acting.

However, if drug dealing occurs on premises for which the professional is accountable, they may themselves be liable for prosecution if they fail to prevent or report it. In general, it is wise to have a policy, publicized clearly to professional workers and to clients, forbidding the possession of or dealing in drugs on any premises for which the professional is responsible, and stating clearly that any such activity will be reported to the police.

In summary, the normal rules of confidentiality apply to revelations by the client that they are using or dealing in drugs. In the vast majority of cases such confessions are made because the client is concerned about these activities and wishes to address them in counselling or therapy. There is no obligation to report such activities to the police, but there may occasionally be times when the counsellor feels that confidentiality should be broken, because of some over-riding public interest. Before doing so, it is wise to consult any professional codes of practice or organizational policies pertaining to the counsellor's work, to seek advice from colleagues, and to seek legal advice, if it is available.

Bill Plummer

* * *

7.2 What can one do if a client is obviously suffering serious harm as result of drug use, but refuses to make changes?

In modern liberal societies, people are not completely free to do as they wish but the freedom of individuals to make decisions for themselves concerning their health and lifestyle is generally regarded as a fundamental right. For example, a person may refuse to accept medical treatment, even if the consequences of that refusal are certain disability or death. If a doctor attempts to treat a patient without the patient's consent, the doctor could be guilty of battery, or could be sued in the civil courts, even if the doctor felt he or she was acting in the patient's best interests.

The main exception to this right to make decisions for oneself is if the person lacks the mental capacity to do so. It is extraordinary that such an important concept as 'capacity' presently has no legal definition. This question was recently examined thoroughly by the Law Commissioners in the United Kingdom, who made a number of detailed recommendations. These included that 'there should be a presumption against lack of capacity' and that questions of capacity should be decided on the balance of probabilities (i.e. people should be assumed to have capacity unless there is reasonably strong evidence to the contrary). Mental incapacity can only occur if there is mental disability, defined as 'any disability or disorder of the mind or brain, whether permanent or temporary, which results in an impairment or disturbance of mental functioning'. Incapacity itself is defined as being unable 'by reason of mental disability to make a decision on the matter in question' or 'unable to communicate a decision on that matter because he is unconscious or for any other reason.'

While someone who abuses drugs or alcohol may temporarily lack mental capacity while intoxicated, there is no doubt that when he or she is in a sober state, according to these definitions they would be assumed to have capacity.

The legal and ethical position is therefore clear. The client has the right to choose whether to continue or not to continue taking drugs or alcohol, whatever the consequences. This is not a decision that the counsellor, therapist or anyone else is entitled to take on the client's behalf. As a corollary to this, it follows that the therapist is not responsible for the consequences of the choices made by the client. It may, however, be personally distressing for the counsellor or therapist to see someone with whom they have formed a close professional relationship suffer serious ill health or other consequences because of the client's lifestyle or decisions.

It is interesting that this question is framed in terms of a 'refusal' to change, rather than in terms of a choice made by the client. It suggests that there may be conflict within the therapeutic relationship. There could simply be competing perspectives, with different views of what is 'best' for the client, or the therapist could perhaps be trying to persuade the client to take a particular course of action, which the client is resisting.

Certainly, what is 'obvious' to the counsellor or therapist may not be at all obvious to the client, who may not be aware of a link between his or her substance misuse and particular consequences. This could be because of ignorance about the effects of drugs or alcohol, or it could be because awareness of the link is being suppressed or denied for emotional reasons. Even if the client is aware of a link between substance misuse and adverse consequences, the client may not wish to change because the predictable and immediate beneficial or rewarding effects of drugs or alcohol may outweigh the less certain and delayed adverse effects. Alternatively, the client may feel unable or incapable of making changes because of previous failed attempts to do so.

It would be worthwhile for the counsellor to explore these possibilities, and to try to understand the client's perceptions and feelings about these issues in greater depth. This is likely to deepen rapport and empathy and strengthen the therapeutic alliance. Paradoxically, this is more likely to lead to positive changes than rational argument or attempts to persuade the client to change.

If there is, indeed, a 'refusal' to change, or a sense of conflict within the therapeutic relationship, it would be worth trying to understand the elements of transference and counter-transference that may be operating. It may, for example, be possible to identify similar repetitive patterns of behaving and relating in the client's (and/or the counsellor's) previous and current relationships. This understanding is likely to help the counsellor cope with this difficult situation, but it is probably not appropriate to work directly with the transference in therapy itself, especially if the therapeutic alliance is already disrupted by conflict.

In fact, this situation is one in which the client almost certainly requires specialist assessment and treatment by addiction services. Indeed, the definition of 'addiction' is that a person continues to use drugs or alcohol in spite of a knowledge of adverse consequences. If possible the counsellor should seek advice from local specialist services or from medical colleagues about how to proceed, or at least should seek the advice of a supervisor or senior colleague. (See also Question 4.8.)

Bill Plummer

* * *

7.3 Can people be forced to accept treatment for their addiction problems, even if they refuse to get help voluntarily?

In principle, the answer to this question is 'No'. People cannot be forced to accept treatment for addiction problems, even if they refuse to get help voluntarily. In practice, there is often a degree of coercion in the background, even when people appear to seek treatment for addictions voluntarily. This may come from the person's employer, family or friends; or other agencies, such as the Courts; or Social Services may be involved. This will usually not make a difference to treatment outcome, as long as the client is able to engage in treatment (rather than simply 'attending' for treatment), and can form a good therapeutic alliance with a counsellor, or with the treatment service as a whole.

On the other hand, there are factors that can be highly disruptive to the formation and maintenance of a therapeutic alliance or prevent the client from taking on personal responsibility for his or her own problems. These include rigid requirements on the client by outside agencies to complete a particular programme of treatment, unrealistic demands that no relapses should occur during the process of treatment, or outside monitoring of the client's 'progress' in treatment. Paradoxically, such attempts to ensure that treatment is effective are likely to undermine the treatment process and result in poorer outcomes.

Substance misuse, particularly alcohol misuse, has for a long time occupied an ill-defined borderland between mental illness and normal behaviour. Addiction is often regarded as an illness, but only sporadic and half-hearted attempts have been made in the past to introduce compulsory treatment. In the case of alcohol, a fascinating account of this is given by Edwards (2000).

The present legal position is that treatment for drug or alcohol abuse is specifically excluded from the provisions of the Mental Health Act 1983, which defines mental disorder as 'mental illness, arrested or incomplete development of mind, psychopathic disorder and any other disorder or disability of mind', but not 'promiscuity or other immoral conduct, sexual deviancy or dependence on alcohol or drugs'. Even if a person is suffering from quite a severe mental disorder, it is not possible to admit him to hospital compulsorily unless certain other criteria apply. He needs to have a mental disorder of 'a nature and degree which warrants the detention of the patient in hospital (for assessment or treatment)'; and he 'ought to be so detained in the interests of his own health or safety or with a view to the protection of other persons'.

The exclusion of drug or alcohol misuse from the Mental Health Act does not mean that mental disorders that arise as a result of substance misuse are excluded from the Act. If a person develops depression and becomes suicidal as a result of substance misuse, the Act would certainly apply, if the above criteria were met. Similarly, if a person develops a drug-induced psychosis or mental confusion, the Act would apply. It is not usual, however, to carry out formal Mental Health Act assessments (which usually require assessment by two independent doctors and a social worker) if the patient is obviously intoxicated with drugs or alcohol. Such assessment is delayed until the acute effects of intoxication have subsided.

Mental health legislation is currently under review, and it is not yet clear how drug or alcohol misuse will be dealt with under any new legislation. In the White Paper *Reforming the Mental Health Act* (Department of Health 2000), a new definition of mental disorder is proposed as 'any disability or disorder of mind or brain, whether permanent or temporary, which results in an impairment or disturbance of mental functioning'. This broad definition is 'intended to ensure that the presence or absence of any one particular clinical condition does not limit the discretion of clinicians to consider whether a patient with mental disorder should be treated under compulsory powers'. Although this definition is broad, it is unlikely that substance misuse would fall within it, but it will be interesting to see the exact wording of any new mental health legislation and how it is interpreted and applied in practice by mental health professionals.

Also of relevance is the European Convention on Human Rights and Fundamental Freedoms, which is a framework for legislation in the member countries of the European Union and has recently been accepted by the United Kingdom. Article Five of this Convention states: 'Everyone has the right to liberty and security of person. No one shall be deprived of this liberty save in the following cases and in accordance with a procedure prescribed by law.' One of the cases is 'the lawful detention of persons of unsound mind'; and this is subject to the conditions that 'everyone who is deprived of his liberty by arrest or detention shall be entitled to take proceedings by which the lawfulness of his detention shall be decided speedily by a court and his release ordered if the detention is not lawful'.

The European Court of Human Rights has established through case law that there are three minimum requirements for a state's mental health legislation to comply with Article Five. The prospective patient 'must be reliably shown by objective medical expertise to be of unsound mind'; the patient's mental disorder 'must be of a kind or degree warranting compulsory confinement'; and 'the unsoundness of mind must continue throughout the period of detention'.

Again, it will be interesting to see how these principles may be applied in future to treatment for drug or alcohol abuse, but it seems unlikely that compulsory hospital treatment could be widely used for substance misuse under these regulations.

Perhaps the commonest situation in which clients suffer some compulsion to attend for treatment is where they have been convicted of a criminal offence, and some form of treatment is included as part of their sentence. The Courts and Probation Services are generally sensible and realistic about this. Probation Services will only recommend and the Courts will only impose such requirements if the convicted person is willing to engage in treatment and there is some likelihood of success.

The Courts have always been able to include such conditions when sentencing, but recently this has been formalized by the introduction of

Drug Testing and Treatment Orders (DTTOs). Under these Orders, people who are convicted of an offence where drug misuse may have been a factor can be required to attend an intensive course of treatment (usually over 20 hours per week), and to submit to repeated testing for drugs. If they fail to attend for treatment at any time, or if they relapse into drug use, the probation service must be informed immediately by the treatment agency, which may also be required to report on the client's progress in treatment.

Clearly, these conditions may make it difficult for either the client or the counsellor to enter wholeheartedly into a therapeutic relationship. For example, the client may fear admitting to certain behaviours because of worries about confidentiality; or the counsellor may not be used to working with rigid requirements for strict abstinence, and may feel uncertain and uncomfortable if required to report to an outside agency.

If possible, it may be helpful to separate the treatment aspects of the programme from any reporting aspects. It may also be possible to negotiate clear boundaries with the client concerning confidentiality.

So far, DTTOs have not been evaluated, and it will be interesting to see how successful they are in practice, whether problems do in fact occur, and what strategies treatment agencies will develop to cope with any difficulties which arise.

Bill Plummer

* * *

7.4 I am concerned that a client is often drunk while in sole charge of his children. Does this mean that the children are 'at risk'?

If a client is often drunk while in sole charge of children, then it is indeed likely that those children are at risk. The main risk they face is of neglect, but they are also at risk of accidents while unsupervised, and they may be at risk of abuse because of the disinhibiting effect of alcohol. This is almost certainly a situation in which the counsellor's duty of confidentiality to the client is outweighed by the 'public interest' in the risk to the children concerned.

On becoming aware of such a risk it would be wise for the counsellor to consult his or her own professional code of conduct, to consult any policies or procedures pertaining to the setting in which he or she works, and to seek the advice of senior colleagues, supervisors or line managers.

A very useful source of advice is the local Social Services, who should provide a facility for anonymous consultation. The client's details do not have to be given at this stage, and the person requesting advice should receive a coded record from Social Services noting the outcome of the consultation. It is important to make a record of this consultation, and of any decisions arising from it, in the client's notes.

Clearly, the concerns of the counsellor should be shared with the client involved, with a view to exploring possible changes in behaviour, including reducing or stopping the episodes of intoxication, or providing more secure and continuous care for the children. It is also crucial to elicit the client's own views and potential concerns. Indeed it is likely that the client is communicating a concern or request for help in bringing these matters to the attention of the counsellor at all.

Possible sources of help and advice for the client should be explored, such as Social Services and the specialist addiction services. The client should be encouraged to seek help voluntarily, although it should be explained that the counsellor may not feel bound by confidentiality in this situation, and that the needs and interests of the children are paramount.

Involvement of Social Services is often frightening for a client, who fears that their children may immediately be taken into care, but it should be seen as an opportunity to access help and support, and to be seen to act responsibly as a parent. Social Services are far less likely to remove children from a carer if that carer acknowledges problems and seeks appropriate help. According to the circumstances, and the nature of the contract with the client, the counsellor may offer to act as an advocate with Social Services, or to be present during any Social Services assessment.

Ultimately, however, if it is felt that a child may be in danger, the counsellor or therapist has a duty to take timely and appropriate action to ensure that the child is protected. In most cases, this will mean informing the local Social Services of these concerns.

Bill Plummer

References

American Psychiatric Association (1994) DSM IV: Diagnostic and Statistical Manual of Mental Disorders, 4th edn. Washington, DC: APA.

Ball SA, Legow NE (1996) Attachment theory as a working model for the therapist transitioning from early to later recovery substance misuse treatment. American Journal of Alcohol Abuse 22(4): 533–47.

Beck AT (1976) Cognitive Therapy and the Emotional Disorders. New York: International Universities Press.

Beck AT, Wright FD, Newman CF, Liese BS (eds) (1993) Cognitive Therapy of Substance Abuse. New York: Guilford.

Bergin AE, Garfield SL (eds) (1994) Handbook of Psychotherapy and Behaviour Change, 4th edn. New York: John Wiley.

Berridge V (1999) Opium and the People: Opium Use and Drug Control Policy in Nineteenth and Early Twentieth Century England. London: Free Association Books.

Berry M (2000) Sexual abuse in childhood. In Feltham C, Horton I (eds), Handbook of Counselling and Psychotherapy. London: Sage Publications.

Bleuler E (1911/1950) Dementia Praecox or the Group of Schizophrenias. New York: International Universities Press.

Bragan K (1996) Self and Spirit in the Therapeutic Relationship. London: Routledge.

Carroll J (1986) Treating multiple substance abuse clients. In Galanter M (ed.), Alcoholism, Vol. 4. New York: Plenum Press.

Cartwright A, Gorman D (1993) Processes involved in changing the therapeutic attitudes of clinicians to working with drinking clients. Psychotherapy Research 3(2): 95–104.

Cartwright A, Hyams G, Spratley T (1996) Is the interviewer's therapeutic commitment an important factor in determining whether alcoholic clients engage in treatment? Addiction Research 4(3): 215–30.

Cartwright AKJ, Kent R, Reading B (1997) The Assessment Interview for Clients with Substance Misuse Problems. Internal publication. Canterbury: The University of Kent.

Cermak T (1989) Al-Anon and recovery in alcoholism. In Galanter M (ed.), Alcoholism, Vol. 7. New York: Plenum Press.

Consumer Reports (1995) Mental health: does therapy help? Consumer Reports 60: 734–39.

Cook CCH, Gurling HMD (2001) Genetic predisposition to alcohol dependence and problems. In Heather N, Peters TJ, Stockwell T (eds), International Handbook of Alcohol Dependence and Problems. Chichester: John Wiley.

Dale P (1999) Adults Abused as Children: Experiences of Counselling and Psychotherapy. London: Sage Publications.

Davidson R (1996) Motivational issues in the treatment of addictive behaviours. In Edwards G, Dare C (eds), Psychotherapy, Psychological Treatments and the Addictions. Cambridge: Cambridge University Press.

Davies JB (2000) The Myth of Addiction. Amsterdam: Harwood Academic Publishers.

Department of Health (2000) Reforming the Mental Health Act. London: Department of Health.

Department of Health (2001) Treatment Choice in Psychological Therapies and Counselling – Evidence-based Clinical Practice Guidelines. London: Department of Health.

Diclemente CC (1991) Motivational interviewing and the stages of change. In Miller WR, Rollnick S (eds), Motivational Interviewing: Preparing People to Change Addictive Behaviour. New York and London: Guilford Press.

Dorn N, Ribbens J, South N (1987) Coping with a Nightmare: Family Feelings About Long-term Drug Use. London: ISDD.

Drummond CD (2001) Theories of drug craving, ancient and modern. Addiction 96: 33–46.

Edwards G (2000) Alcohol: The Ambiguous Molecule. London: Penguin.

Edwards G, Dare C (1996) Psychotherapy, Psychological Treatments and the Addictions. Cambridge: Cambridge University Press.

Edwards G, Marshall EJ, Cook CH (eds) (1997) The Treatment of Drinking Problems. Cambridge: Cambridge University Press.

Ellis A, McInerney J, DiGuiseppe R, Yeager R (1988) Rational Emotive Therapy with Alcoholics and Substance Abusers. Boston, MA: Allyn and Bacon.

Finkelhor D, Browne A (1986) A Source Book on Child Sexual Abuse. London: Sage Publications.

Guntrip H (1969) Schizoid Phenomena, Object Relations and the Self. New York: International Universities Press.

Hall L, Lloyd S (1989) Surviving Child Sexual Abuse. Lewes: The Falmer Press.

Harris P (2001) Concrete counselling. Druglink 16: 10–13.

Heather N (1992) Addictive disorders are essentially motivational problems. British Journal of Addiction 87: 828–30.

Heather N (1996) The effectiveness of treatment for alcohol problems: a matter of interpretation. Journal of Substance Misuse 1: 126–31.

Heather N, Robertson I (1983) Controlled Drinking. 2nd edn. London: Methuen.

Heron J (1990) Helping the Client: A Creative and Practical Guide. London: Sage Publications.

Hester RK, Miller WR (eds) (1989) Handbook of Alcoholism Treatment Approaches: Effective Alternatives, 2nd edn. Boston, MA: Allyn and Bacon.

Horvath AO, Symonds BD (1991) Relation between working alliance and outcome in psychotherapy: a meta-analysis. Journal of Counseling Psychology 38: 139–49.

Hubble M, Duncan B, Miller S (eds) (1999) The Heart and Soul of Change: What Works in Therapy. Washington, DC: American Psychological Association.

Jackson P (1996) When there are two clients in a session. Addiction Counselling World 7: 39.

Jackson P (1997) Using pharmacology in counselling. Addiction Counselling World, 9(49): 21–23.

Jackson P (2000a) Remotivate disillusioned carers. Addiction Today 11: 63.

Jackson P (2000b) The transtheoretical approach. In Feltham C, Horton I (eds), Handbook of Counselling and Psychotherapy. London: Sage Publications.

Jackson P (2001) Relationships: is alcohol your partner? Addiction Today 13(72): 14–15.

Karpman S (1968) Fairy tales and script drama analysis. Transactional Analysis Bulletin 7(26): 29–33.

Keene J (1997) Drug Misuse: Prevention, Harm Minimisation and Treatment. London: Chapman and Hall.

Kent R (1995) Talking it Through – the National Alcohol Concern Vocational Training Pack. London: Alcohol Concern.

Kinney J, Montgomery M (1979) Psychotherapy and the member of Alcoholics Anonymous. In Galanter M (ed.), Alcoholism, Vol. 6. New York: Grune and Stratton.

Leiper R, Kent R (2001) Working through Setbacks in Psychotherapy – Crisis, Impasse and Relapse. London: Sage Publications.

Lemert E (1966) Human Deviance, Social Problems and Social Control. Englewood Cliffs, NJ: Prentice Hall.

Luborsky L (1984) Principles of Psychoanalytic Psychotherapy: A Manual for Supportive–Expressive Treatment. New York: Basic Books.

Luborsky L, McLellan AT, Woody GE, O'Brien CP, Auerbach A (1986) Therapists' success and its determinants. Archives of General Psychiatry 42: 602–11.

Macdonald D, Patterson V (1991) A Handbook of Drug Training. London: Routledge.

McMurran M (1994) The Psychology of Addiction. London: Taylor and Francis.

Marlatt A, Gordon JR (1985) Relapse Prevention. New York: Guilford.

Miller WR (1983) Motivational interviewing with problem drinkers. Behavioural Psychotherapy 11: 147–72.

Miller WR (1985) Motivation for treatment: a review with special emphasis on alcoholism. Psychological Bulletin 98: 84–107.

Miller WR, Baca LM (1983) Two-year follow-up of bibliotherapy and therapist-directed controlled drinking for problem drinkers. Behaviour Therapy 14: 441–48.

Miller WR, Munoz RF (1982) How to Control Your Drinking, revd edn. Albuquerque, NM: University of New Mexico Press.

Miller WR, Rollnick S (eds) (1991) Motivational Interviewing: Preparing People to Change Addictive Behaviours. New York and London: Guilford Press.

Miller WR, Taylor CA, West JC (1980) Focussed vs. broad-spectrum behavior therapy for problem drinkers. Journal of Consulting and Clinical Psychology 48: 590–601.

Nace EP (1987) The Treatment of Alcoholism. New York: Brunner/Mazel.

Najavits L, Weiss RD (1994) Variations in therapist effectiveness in the treatment of patients with substance use disorders: an empirical view. Addiction 89: 679–88.

Newcombe R (1992) The reduction of drug related harm: a conceptual framework for theory, practice and research. In O'Hare P, Newcombe R, Matthews A, Buning EC, Drucker E (eds), The Reduction of Drug-related Harm. London: Routledge.

Norcross JC, Prochaska JO (1983) Clinicians' theoretical orientations: selection, utilisation and efficacy. Professional Psychology: Research and Practice 14(2): 197–208.

NTORS (1996) The National Treatment Outcome Study. London: Department of Health.

Orford J (1999) Future research directions: a commentary on project MATCH. Addiction 94(1): 62–66.

Orford J (2001) Excessive Appetites: A Psychological View of Addictions. Chichester: John Wiley.

Premack D (1970) Mechanisms of self control. In Hunt WA (ed.), Learning Mechanisms in Smoking. Chicago: Aldine.

Prochaska JO, Diclemente CC (1986) Toward a comprehensive model of change. In Miller WR, Heather N (eds), Treating Addictive Behaviours. New York: Plenum Press.

Prochaska JO, Diclemente CC (1992) The transtheoretical approach. In Norcross JC, Goldfried MR (eds), Handbook of Psychotherapy Integration. New York: Basic Books.

Project MATCH (1997) Matching alcoholism treatments to client heterogeneity: Project MATCH post-treatment outcomes. Journal of Studies on Alcohol 58(1): 7–29.

Reading B (2001) The application of Bowlby's Attachment Theory to psychotherapy in the addictions. In Weegmann M, Cohen E (eds), Psychodynamics of Addiction. London: Whurr Publishers.

Robins LN (1974) The Vietnam Drug User Returns. Special Action Office Monograph, Series A, No. 2. Washington DC: US Government Printing Office.

Rollnick S, Bell A (1991) Brief motivational interviewing for use by the non-specialist. In Miller WR, Rollnick S (eds), Motivational Interviewing: Preparing People to Change Addictive Behaviour. New York and London: Guilford Press.

Rollnick S, Miller W (1995) What is motivational interviewing? Behavioural and Cognitive Psychotherapy 23: 325–34.

Rogers CR (1957) The necessary and sufficient conditions of therapeutic personality change. Journal of Consulting Psychology 21: 95–103.

Rogers C (1987) Client Centred Therapy. London: Constable.

Roth A, Fonagy P (1996) What Works for Whom? New York: Guilford Press.

Russell MAH (1976) What is dependence? In Edwards G, Russell G, Hawks MAH, MacCarthy D (eds), Drugs and Drugs Dependence. Lexington, MA: Saxon House.

Saunders B, Wilkinson C, Allsop S (1991) Motivational interviewing with heroin users attending a methadone clinic. In Miller WR, Rollnick S (eds), Motivational Interviewing: Preparing People to Change Addictive Behaviours. New York and London: Guilford Press.

Schachter M (1993) Psychotherapy and Medication: A Dynamic Integration. New Jersey: Jason Aronson.

Seligman M (1995) The effectiveness of psychotherapy – the Consumer Reports Study. American Psychologist 50(12): 965–74.

Stimson GV (2000) Blair declares war: the unhealthy state of British drug policy. International Journal of Drug Policy 11(4): 259-64.

Sutton S (1996) Can 'stages of change' provide guidance in the treatment of addictions? A critical examination of Prochaska and Diclemente's model. In Edwards G, Dare C (eds), Psychotherapy, Psychological Treatments and the Addictions. Cambridge: Cambridge University Press.

Tiebout H (1944) Therapeutic mechanisms of Alcoholics Anonymous. American Journal of Psychiatry 100: 468–73.

Valle SK (1981) Interpersonal functioning of alcoholism counsellors and treatment outcome. Journal of Studies on Alcohol 42(9): 783–90.

Velleman R (1992) Counselling for Alcohol Problems. London: Sage Publications.

Walton S (2001) Out of it: A Cultural History of Intoxication. London: Hamish Hamilton.

Weegmann M (2001) Psychodynamic assessment of drug addicts. In Weegmann M, Cohen R (eds), Psychodynamics of Addiction. London: Whurr Publishers.

Weinberg BA, Bealer BK (2001) The World of Caffeine: The Science and Culture of the World's Most Popular Drug. New York: Routledge.

White W (1993) Critical Incidents: Ethical Issues in Substance Abuse Prevention and Treatment. Bloomington, IL: Lighthouse Training Institute.

Wurmser L (ed.) (1978) The Hidden Dimension: Psychodynamics in Compulsive Drug Use. New York: Jason Aronson.

Index